For Women By Women

Financial Passages

FIRST EDITION

To all the women who have touched my life,
especially my grandmothers,
who helped pave the way for us all.

Contents

Chapter One
What is Financial Planning?
—Lois Carrier, CFP™

Most people spend more time planning their vacations than they spend planning for their futures. In this chapter, Lois describes the various parts of the financial plan, including the major investment classes and the factors that affect them.

Chapter Two
Couplehood and Parenthood
—Barbara Culver, CFP™

The passage to couplehood and the passage to parenthood are choices that can have enormous financial components. In this chapter, Barbara raises issues that need to be considered by any woman who is thinking about sharing her life with another person.

Parents who have children with special needs spend much time and energy on creating a life that accommodates those needs. Often, parents are so busy with resolving crises in their immediate future that they do not explore what needs to be done for their child after they pass away. In this chapter, Roberta explains the primary financial planning issues facing parents who have children with special needs.

The passage into your employment life begins a chain of events that will shape your eventual retirement. In this chapter, Carter explains the challenges women face and describes the common vehicles we can use to help maximize our pre-retirement dollars.

The passage through divorce—no matter who initiated it—is accompanied by financial changes that must be contemplated within an emotional climate. That emotional climate can make it very difficult to make rational, productive decisions for your future. In this chapter, Cicily focuses on the process of divorce, explaining what you need to know, what you need to think about, and whom you need to hire to help you.

Acknowledgments

I want to thank the following people for helping in the production of this book: my co-workers at Resonate Inc. for their support and encouragement, Maryterasa Martin for professional guidance and patient nudging, and Dan Betzel and Dave Kauffman for their insightful discussions.

Introduction

The topic of money is largely taboo in many cultures, especially for women. Although we Americans are more open than many cultures, we still shy away from discussing personal financial details. In fact, many women seem to be painfully unclear about the role of money in our lives. After all, we don't talk about how much we earn or how much we are *worth*. And what's worse, we often confuse *self-worth* with *net worth*, believing that the number of zeros in our balance sheet is an indication of our importance.

Many of us allow money—or our perceived need for it—to control us. We do this by overspending or spending inappropriately. We feel guilty when we spend money and angry or resentful when we don't. We use money to buy "stuff" to make us feel good or look good to others. We don't realize that we are using money to express feelings we cannot speak of—or that we cannot even identify.

Our motivation for writing this book was to give women the guidance they need to financially empower themselves. All five of us have survived different hardships and enjoyed different successes, but together we have shared this vision.

Our professional lives are dedicated to increasing the financial literacy of women. That includes educating women about the affect that their feelings and their experiences have on their finances. Our collaboration grew out of our desire to help women solve problems, avoid mistakes and deal appropriately with crises.

Part of solving problems is recognizing them and then seeking help. Financial problems are no exception and we all recommend enlisting the help of an expert when dealing with them. More important, we recommend enlisting the help of an expert when dealing with any major passage in your life that involves money. Why? Because along with money issues come tax issues, planning issues and even emotional issues.

It is an awesome experience to join with four other CERTIFIED FINANCIAL PLANNER practitioners, each an expert in a particular field and yet knowledgeable in many planning areas. We all have within us the power to become financially literate and financially independent. And we owe it to ourselves—and our children—to become masters of our financial lives so that we may pass that financial intelligence on to them.

We hope you enjoy this book and learn from our knowledge and experience.

Lois Carrier, CFP™
Barbara Culver, CFP™
Carter Leinster, CFP™
Cicily Maton, CFP™
Roberta Welsh, CFP™

Chapter One

What is Financial Planning?

By Lois Carrier, CFP™

Going on Vacation?

Would you consider traveling to someplace new without consulting a map? Not if you were going to make effective use of your time and see what you wanted to see. Your optimal strategy would be to choose the places you wanted to visit, locate them on your map, and note where they were in relation to where you were going to stay. You'd determine the best path to take, and decide if it would be best to walk, take a cab, or take some form of mass transportation. You'd write down your plan, but you'd be aware that if the weather wasn't cooperating, or if for some other reason you weren't able to do what you had originally planned when you had originally planned to do it, you'd have to revise your itinerary a bit to accommodate whatever had occurred.

Fortunately, most people know that this is the best way to plan their vacations. Unfortunately, most people plan more for their two-week vacation than they do for their financial journey through life.

The Plan

Building your personal wealth is a process that usually takes decades. In the meantime, you need to take steps that will lead you toward your future goals, while providing for your present needs.

A financial plan shows you what each step on your personal financial journey should look like. As your life evolves and your circumstances change, your financial plan changes accordingly. Your financial plan is organic; it evolves in tandem with your life.

Your Plan

What are your present and future financial needs and desires? Have you written all of them down? Do you have a practical plan for achieving them? For instance, do you know how much money you need to put away, and how much you need to earn on that money in order to reach your present and future goals? Do you know what kinds of insurance you need? Do you have an estate plan?

These are the questions that CERTIFIED FINANCIAL PLANNER practitioners help their clients answer. Individual investors choose CFPs as their advisors because they are trained to take care of almost all of their clients' personal finance needs. Another reason is the way in which CFPs are compensated—on a fee basis rather than commission. In other words, you can be sure that the investment advice you are getting is not generated by the planner's potential commission.

Finding a Financial Planner

If you wanted to find an accountant or an attorney, what would you do? Assuming you didn't have one in the family and none of your friends had been singing the praises of their accountant or attorney, you'd probably ask the friends of yours who appear to be most content with their lives. Why? Because people who are "together" usually know other people who are "together."

If you ask around and don't get any referrals, go for referrals of referrals. What I mean is that good attorneys usually know good accountants, and both usually know good financial planners.

And if those queries don't get you anywhere, or if you prefer to do your own research, you can find a good planner with the help of a phone book and your local newspaper.

The Phone Book

Look under "financial planners" in the yellow pages, and look through the list.
If you don't get a particularly warm and fuzzy feeling about any of the ads or names (don't discount your intuition—it is usually correct), just start calling in search of the following information:

- Describe yourself and your needs and see if there's a fit. If, for example, you are a self-employed, single mother who is interested in stepping-up saving for her children's educations, and who would also like to explore her insurance needs, you might not want to go to a man whose specialty is corporate retirement plans. In other words, you want to go to someone who works with clients like you.
- If there seems to be a fit, ask if there is a fee for an initial consultation. This information alone should not make your decision; you are asking because you want to know exactly what you are dealing with.
- Make enough calls so you have a list of three or four planners to meet with. Although you might get a good feeling or a bad feeling from your initial phone call, remember that you have no idea what was going on in that person's life at the time you were speaking. Everyone has great moments, and everyone has especially horrible moments within an otherwise happy day. Don't judge anyone based on one conversation—particularly one conducted over the phone.
- Make a checklist of all of the things that are important to you in your optimal relationship with your financial planner. No one will have all of them, but this exercise helps you establish what you need and what you can do without. In my experience, the top concern of most women is that they feel comfortable with the level of communication. You want to be able to feel comfortable asking all types of questions and asking for clarification, and even asking for re-clarification. You don't want to ever work with someone who makes you feel less-than-intelligent, capable, and valued.
- Ask for references: preferably people who have a situation similar to yours. And call those references. Remember, you are entrusting this person with your financial present and future; this is not a decision to take lightly.

Your Local Newspapers

How can your local newspaper help you with your search for a financial planner? In the classified ads and in your local Pennysaver, you will see ads for seminars given by local financial planners. If you have the time, go to one. You are bound to learn something and you might even like the presenter and decide to look into hiring her/him. My only caveat is not to make your decision to work with someone based on watching one seminar. Make an appointment to meet with the person to ascertain whether she/he is a good fit for you.

What To Do Before Your First Appointment

Before you interview any financial planners, you should do a bit of planning for those meetings. All planners you interview will want to know what your general situation is, and any specifics you can provide. The more you know about your own financial life, the better the interviewee will be able to help you. These are among the things you should know about your financial life:

- What is your monthly/annual income?
- What are its sources?
- When does it arrive?
- Is it taxable?
- What are your monthly expenses?
- What kind of insurance(s) do you have?
- What kinds of investments do you have, and what returns have you been getting?
- What are your short, intermediate, and long-term goals?
- Do you have a living will?
- Do you have a will?
- Do you have an estate plan?

If you cannot answer these questions, chances are your financial plan is either non-existent, or not sufficient.

However, that's why you need a financial planner. If all you had to do during the day was manage your investments to accommodate the changes in your life while keeping up with your objectives, you wouldn't need help. But most women in this third millennium have plenty to do each day, and thinking about the minutiae of their financial plans usually is not at the top of their list of priorities.

In addition, financial planning is a rational discipline based on sound principles that have been effective for decades. Contrastingly, your financial life is always tightly tied to your emotional life, and can easily be influenced by it. Many people, once their emotions are triggered, find it difficult to make rational decisions. This tends to be the case especially immediately after the event that triggered the emotion (let's say a divorce). Your financial planner should be keenly aware of the relationship between emotions and finances, and should be able to keep you on track. She should also be able to anticipate problems and guide you through the financial part of your emotional life.

What about other types of financial advisors?

The authors of this book are all CERTIFIED FINANCIAL PLANNERs. Our professional education was designed to prepare us to deal with a client's entire financial landscape and all of the variables that affect it. The variables include emotions, taxes, family relations, career changes, and other aspects of your life that directly impact your present and future finances.

Many other financial services professionals have seen the benefit of this holistic perspective and have changed the way they do business. For this reason, it is more important than ever to ask any financial advisor you are interviewing what their philosophy is. You want them to explain how they would approach your financial life.

Another aspect of financial planning that many other financial services professionals are transitioning to, is fee-based money management. In other words, when they started their business, it was mostly commission-based. This was great for them, but the concept of commission always makes the client question whether the advisor's recommendation is completely based on the client's interests. Increasingly more consumers are choosing fee-based advisors over those who are commission-based just for that reason.

There are many financial services professionals who do not have the CERTIFIED FINANCIAL PLANNER designation and who do much of what we do and are even compensated the way we are. They may be harder to find, but they are out there. This is why the interview is so important. If you'd like to broaden your search to non-CFPs, just be sure to ask how they will approach your situation. Remember that you want someone who will factor in all the parts of your financial landscape, whose compensation structure is one you agree with, and who communicates with you in a way you find satisfactory.

Your Portfolio: What It Is and What Affects It

When you decide on a financial planner, you will meet with that person to talk about more than just your money; you will talk about your life. After all, the needs that you have from your money are based on your life's events that concern money. If you think about it, most of your life's major events will indeed involve money. For instance:

- Purchasing a home
- Getting married
- Retirement
- Divorce (which is likely to alter your financial situation one way or the other)
- The death of your partner or spouse
- Sending your children to private school and/or college

All of these items have a significant financial element. They probably have varying timetables, and they all involve different financial levels, but none of them are easily dealt with in the absence of a plan.

No matter how many life events you anticipate, there will still be some that take you by surprise. The idea is to plan as thoroughly as possible for what you expect, and be flexible enough to embrace the idea of altering your plans if you and your planner agree you need to. This is easier for some people than it is for others, and each situation is unique and warrants much personal contemplation and an open mind.

The Basic Vocabulary of Financial Planning

Though the details of your unique life dictate the details of your unique financial plans, there are some fundamentals that need to know. They are the same fundamentals that even the wealthiest people need to know in order to confidently take charge of their personal finances and ensure their financial security.

Your *portfolio* is, essentially, your money. More specifically, it is a group of investments that are chosen by you and your planner because they are appropriate for the short (the next five years), intermediate (five to ten years from now) and long-term more than 10 years from now) goals you have created for yourself.

Your investments will be chosen from various asset classes that have different returns and different levels of *risk*. In general, the higher the risk involved in an investment, the higher the potential *return*. Savvy investing (and savvy investment advice) is a matter of choosing investments that will provide you with the funds you need (and preferably more), when you need them, without assuming an amount of risk that you are uncomfortable with.

The concept of putting a percentage of your money into different investments that have different rates of return and different degrees of risk associated with them is called *asset allocation*. The basic *asset classes* that asset allocation refers to are *cash, stocks, bonds* and *mutual funds*. First, I'll further define these concepts, then I'll review a part of financial life that is often overlooked: your basic insurance needs.

Risk

Risk is an important concept to examine and understand. Let me begin by saying that every investment has risk; it's a matter of degree and type. For instance, the risk of certificates of deposit (CDs, in the asset class *cash*), which are considered "safe" investments, is that inflation will destroy the purchasing power of the money you have invested over time. This risk exists because CDs offer low interest rates that are fixed, while the inflation rate is not static. In other words, if you have all of your money in CDs, and the interest rate rises to, say, 8% and stays there, when it is time to get your money, it could actually be worth less than when you purchased the CDs. I've heard CDs referred to as a way to lose money safely.

Another kind of risk you need to think about is known as *business risk*. This simply means that a company you invest in could go out of business. If, for example, you invest all of your money in XYZ corporation and it goes out of business, where does that leave you? Not in a very good place. If, however, you invest all of your money in one mutual fund that owns shares of XYZ corporation in addition to shares of sixty other companies, and XYZ goes out of business, where are you now? Later I will discuss stocks and mutual funds in more detail and you will see that the best way to handle risk, in general, is to diversify your portfolio by not putting too much money in any one investment.

Probably the most distressing, yet least understood type of risk, is known as *market risk*, and it pertains to the stock market. Most people think of risk only in terms of loss. However if risk is loss, then everyone is risk averse. After all, no one wants to lose money. But when it comes to the stock market, the potential for loss does not stop at money.

The stock market is volatile; it goes up and down, and sometimes very quickly and very steeply. This has always been the case and will always be the case. Unfortunately, not every investor is up to the emotional ups and downs that accompany the financial ones. Money and emotions are connected and affect each other more than most people realize. A common sequence of events is:

- The market goes down sharply.
- Your emotions follow (you doubt yourself and your choices, you begin to wonder if you will make your financial goals, perhaps you blame your advisor and become angry).
- You lose sleep (or get too much).
- You gain weight (or lose some).
- You argue with your spouse, children, and co-workers.
- Your skin breaks out.
- You begin to make bad decisions (financial and otherwise) because of the above.

The above scenario is not uncommon during times of volatility in the stock market. The problem is we do not know when those times will be the worst. This is why it is vital for you to discuss the various types of risk with your planner and determine which ones you are willing to take, and to what degree.

How do you respond to risk?

One of the first things your planner will probably want to do is establish your risk tolerance. This assessment usually takes the form of a questionnaire that is designed to determine how much stress you can handle when it comes to your investments and the things that affect them. Let me explain further.

I've said that the different asset classes come with different levels of risk. For instance, we all know that the stock market goes up and down, up and down. That is the risk you assume when you invest in stocks. That's fine in theory. But if *you* had all of *your* money in the stock market, I can say with certainty that you would be happier when it was going up, and quite distraught when it took a plunge. Your mood, and in turn your life, would be affected. That is not a position anyone wants to be in.

I don't know any financial planners who advise their clients to put all of their money in the stock market, for that precise reason. Instead, financial planners work with the risk tolerance of the client (defined as low, moderate, or high) and diversify their portfolio to help minimize risk. *Diversification* is the allocation of funds over the various investment classes in such a way as to spread the risk associated with them. For instance, if you were risk averse, meaning your tolerance for risk is low, you would put more money in bonds (typically a lower risk investment) than you would in stocks (higher risk investments).

Furthermore, within the investment classes, there is also a variety of risk levels. Within the asset class known as stocks, there are various types, and some have more risk than others. For example, blue chip stocks are known for their stability—their predictability. Meanwhile, biotechnology stocks and technology stocks are more volatile. The stability makes the blue chips a lower risk investment than the biotechnology and the technology stocks.

So if you are risk averse, yet you still want to be involved in the stock market in order to combat inflation, you would invest in stocks such as blue chips. And if you absolutely wanted to be involved in companies researching alternatives to the current treatments for cancer, yet you were risk averse, you would stay away from the biotech companies and invest in pharmaceuticals, which tend to be larger, older, more stable companies.

Inflation—A Powerful Motivation For Taking Risks

Inflation is one of the most serious threats to your financial security because it constantly gnaws at your purchasing power. Think for a moment about a postage stamp. In 1974, you could purchase a postage stamp for ten cents. In 2000, a stamp costs 33 cents. In 26 years, the cost increased over 300%! How many retirees do you know whose incomes have more than tripled during that same period of time? Inflation can be compared to termites that eat away at the solid foundation of a house. Too often, the damage can't be seen until it's too late.

The way to combat inflation is to make sure that the investments you choose have a rate of return that is higher than inflation. Naturally, you want to get the highest rate of return you possibly can, so you go for the asset with that has outperformed inflation better than any other (stocks), right? Not necessarily. If it were that easy, we'd all have all of our money in the stock market and there would be no need for financial planners.

This is where the artistry of financial planning enters the picture. Recall that the different asset classes have different risks associated with them. And they also have different rates of return. The optimal investment for everyone would be a low risk investment that has a high rate of return. Unfortunately, however, low risk investments usually have lower rates of return *because* you are not taking much risk when you buy them. It's logical that if you were going to take a big risk, the only reason you would consider doing so would be if you had the potential for a big return.

Risk and Timelines

The timeline for your objectives for your money will determine where you invest it. The discussion regarding risk, inflation and rate of return is complete only in the context of your list of life objectives that involve money. And that list is complete only if each item has a time period attached to it. The standard way of looking at your goals is short, intermediate and long-term. Naturally, whether a goal is short, intermediate, or long-term depends on your age, your present financial status, and when you will need the money. I recommend drafting a set of objectives before you visit your financial planner so your time is better spent and more focused.

Diversification and Asset Allocation

The best way to minimize your exposure to the various types of risk (and note that I didn't say avoid them, because every investment has some kind of risk) is to diversify your portfolio. This means that you want to avoid putting all of your proverbial eggs in one basket. Diversification is tied to asset allocation. Diversification is the goal you want to achieve, and you do it by allocating your assets in a way that factors in your risk tolerance as well as your investment objectives and their time horizons. The asset allocation model that is right for you, then, will depend on your unique life and circumstances.

Your *asset allocation* is essentially the percentage of the total amount you are investing that will go into cash, stocks, bonds and mutual funds. There are other investments, such as insurance, real estate, and annuities that you might purchase, and I will touch on those as well. Most people can achieve all of their investment objectives with cash (CDs, money market accounts, and savings accounts) stocks, bonds and mutual funds.

Historically, most asset classes have done well over a five-year period of time. That is why investing should not be considered for short-term objectives. Any asset class could drop for two or three years in a row. But, over a five-year cycle, most classes have recovered and returned to their long-term averages.

The stock market has been down an average of one out of every three years (the "two steps forward, one step back" asset). However, over the long-term, stocks are the only asset that have consistently outperformed the other classes as well as outpacing inflation.

Therefore, an efficient portfolio for everyone would be to use cash (i.e., CDs, money market accounts and savings accounts) for short-term objectives, and stocks for long-term objectives (more than 10 years away). As for intermediate-term objectives (between five and ten years from now), your investments would depend on just how aggressive your disposition is, and how much risk you can handle.

Let's examine the asset classes, the risks involved with them, and other major issues you should be acquainted with in order to maximize your time with your financial planner.

Cash

When you deposit your paycheck into your savings or checking account, you can say, with near certainty, that if you want to withdraw any of those funds at any time, you could. Cash, as an asset class, is composed of several investments that act just like the money you deposited from your paycheck. In other words, you are certain that the amount you deposited will be available for withdrawal (i.e., there is little *risk to your principal*), you might even get a bit more (i.e., interest), and you can get your money at a moment's notice, whenever you please (i.e., it has a high level of *liquidity*).

Generally speaking, investments in the cash class offer similar safety of principal, a bit of interest (some more than others), and a high level of liquidity. Some examples of investments known as cash are:

- Passbook savings accounts (i.e., savings accounts that are not also checking accounts)
- Certificates of deposit (CDs)
- Money market deposit accounts
- Money market funds
- U.S. Government Series EE bonds (more on bonds later)
- U.S. Treasury bills

As an asset class, cash is an investment that you would want to use for your short-term objectives. For instance, if you wanted to go on a vacation next year or if you or your child were getting married in a year or two, you would keep the money you needed in cash. The reason for this is you want to make sure you ended up with at least the same amount you put in. And if you had some kind of emergency between now and your vacation or the wedding, you could withdraw any or all of your funds without penalty.

Notice the implication that cash investments do not grow your money much. And notice that the low growth potential comes with low risk; you are certain your principal will not decrease. But that principal might not have maintained its purchasing power while it was invested. The best way to grow your money—if you can handle the risks associated with it and you can invest it for at least ten years—is to invest in the stock market.

Stocks

Stocks are also referred to as equities. Just as homeowners own the equity in their homes, stockholders own equity in the company whose stock they own. A helpful analogy is to think of a company's total shares of stock as an apple pie. A slice of the apple pie would be a share of stock (also known as *equity*). If the pie were divided into twelve slices, and you bought one slice, you would own one twelfth of the pie.

And although each of those slices is similar, they are not all created equal. Some stocks are purchased because of their *growth*, meaning the company's earnings are likely to rise and the price of the stock will rise with it. Others are purchased for *income*, meaning they are not likely to grow as fast but they do offer their shareholders dividends on a scheduled (perhaps quarterly) basis. Yet others are purchased for their *value*. Value stocks are good companies that aren't doing as well as they could be (so they are not selling at their highs and are relatively inexpensive), but are likely to recover. These pay dividends and show promise of capital gains. The type of stock you purchase will depend on your risk tolerance as well as what you are trying to accomplish.

Where Stocks Are Traded

Companies are publicly held, meaning shares are available to the general public, or privately held, meaning they are not. The public companies trade their stock at various stock exchanges around the world, such as the New York Stock Exchange (NYSE) and "over the counter" (OTC) with the NASDAQ (National Association of Security Dealers Automated Quotation system).

The most obvious difference between NASDAQ and the NYSE is that the NYSE is a physical space where people who represent the public companies meet with people who represent institutions who wish to buy and sell large numbers of shares of the companies. They do their business on the trading floor, in an atmosphere somewhat like a bazaar, where there is much haggling. When you are watching part of a broadcast on CNBC or another financial network and they broadcast from "the floor," you are looking at live action at the New York Stock Exchange. The NASDAQ, on the other hand, is completely computer-based; you cannot locate it in space.

Making the Best of Stocks

The way to make money from stocks is to buy them when their price is low, hold them until the price rises, and then sell them. This is what "buy low, sell high" refers to, and it is a sound investment philosophy that no financial planner will disagree with it. However, it is not always easy to stick to. For example . . .

You are watching a financial segment of a news show and you hear about the newest technology stock to triple in price during the course of a month, reaching an all-time high. You just might be tempted to invest in it, thinking that it will probably keep going higher. Essentially, you are planning at that moment to buy the stock at its highest price ever. Then what? Here are the possibilities over the next month:

- It doesn't go any higher. Would you sell it? If so, when?
- It keeps going higher. Would you sell it? If so, when?
- It goes up and down. Would you sell it? If so, when?

Here's another example . . .

The stock of a well-known, stable company is falling because of, let's say, a judgment against them. It's probable, according to the experts, that when the dust settles, the price of the stock will go back up. You'd like to invest. What do you do? You wait until the price is its lowest, and then you invest before it goes back up, right? Right. The only problem is that you don't know when that is going to happen. Nor does your financial planner. This phenomenon is often referred to as "trying to catch a falling knife," and I do not recommend it.

Both of the stories above raise two major topics in financial planning: market timing, and the need for a *personal investment philosophy*.

Many people claim to be able to know, either psychically or through a secret mathematical theorem, when the market is going to go up or down. "Timing the market" is the alleged ability to determine, in advance, the optimal moment to get out of the market or a stock, and the optimal moment to go back in. The purpose of market timing, then, is to be positioned to benefit when the market shoots up, and to not lose money when it crashes. You go in at the precisely right moment, make some money, and get out at the precise moment you need to to avoid losing money. While this is a truly brilliant idea, *no market timer in the history of the stock market has ever been correct on a consistent basis.*

Because the reality is that market timing isn't possible, the way to build wealth is by a *personal investment philosophy* that is sound and appropriate for your unique life and circumstances. Your financial planner will discuss the details at length with you. For now, be aware that an investment philosophy is necessary because it keeps you in line when you might be tempted to do something impulsive or irresponsible.

For instance, let's say part of your investment philosophy is to *buy and hold* your stocks. This means your focus is not on heavy trading (buying and selling), and you are investing in good, solid companies that are likely to grow and become more valuable over time. If you are committed to this philosophy, when one of your stocks dips along with the rest of the market, you won't sell it. Usually.

The other part of the *buy and hold* idea is that you want to set criteria for selling an investment and for buying additional shares. For this reason, you and your planner might create a plan that includes parameters for what you will do when a specific investment drops in price. For example, you might agree to limit the amount of losses by *selling* if the price goes dips 20% from the price at which you purchased it. And for buying additional shares of a high-quality company you own at a much lower price than its current market price, you might create a plan to *buy* more shares if the price dips 10%. This is known as buying on sale, which is as good an idea in the stock market as it is at your favorite department store.

The details of your philosophy will be customized by you and your planner to accommodate your unique needs. Whatever they are, it is important that you follow them diligently and not allow anyone (e.g., your sister-in-law with the hot stock tip) or anything (e.g., your emotions) to cause you to deviate from your plan.

The Behavior of The Stock Market

I've said that the market will continue to go up and down. When it drops more than 20%, that is called a crash, and when it drops 10% that is called a *correction*. When the stock market downturns continuously for a year or more, that is called a *bear market* (as opposed to a *bull market*, which is a continuous rise). These are all normal events, and there has never been a time when our economy has not recovered from downturns. Although, past performance is no guarantee of future results.

There have been *individuals* who have not recovered, and I'll explain why. Let's consider the stock market crash of October 19, 1987. The people who actually lost money were those who wanted to get out of the market "before they lost any more money." The flaw in that thinking, however, is that the only reason they actually lost money was *because* they got out.

An important fact to remember regarding stock market volatility is that if the market plummets and all of your stocks drop 90% in value, that does not mean you have lost any money. You would only lose money if you panicked and sold all of your stocks because of the crash. If you remind yourself that the stock market has always rebounded and soared to new highs, and you are patient during the rebound process, you are less likely to lose money. If you are the kind of person who tends to panic, and/or if you have a history of being very impatient, your planner will probably advise you to invest only in the lower risk stock mutual funds.

Before labeling yourself risk-averse and refusing to put any money in the stock market, make sure you understand the risks you assume by *not* being in the stock market. Let's go back to the stock market crash in 1987. Many individuals panicked and got out, losing everything along the way. But while they were selling, others were buying. For example, companies were buying their own stocks, and at all-time low prices. They knew the market would go back up, and it did, in less than three months. And in less than three months they made huge profits.

Savvy investors know that when a stock is on sale, they should buy it. I have always found it interesting that most people want to buy at bargain prices unless it's a stock that's on sale. Stocks with all-time highs look far more appealing. But if a stock is at an all-time high, and you don't own it, you are too late. Instead, you should assess whether you think it is worth the all-time high price, and if you do, wait until it goes down and buy it with the hope that it will go back up.

You may ask, "What if the market crashes and doesn't go back up?" It won't matter. If the stock market crashes and doesn't go back up, then nothing matters. If that happens, our country is gone! Even banks with our "safe money," such as money market accounts and savings accounts will be gone too. As long as we have a country and an economy, the stock market will climb again. After all, the stock market represents almost everything material that we need to live our lives the way we do in America. As long as we need those things, the stock market will climb.

Bonds

Bonds are what are known as debt instruments. This means that they are tools corporations and governments use to borrow the money they need (from you) for various projects. When you purchase a bond, you are lending money to the corporation or government, for a specified period of time (anywhere from six months to thirty years or more). In turn, they provide you with periodic interest payments (also stated in advance), until the bond is *due* (and that date is referred to as the bond's *maturity date*). It can also be *called*, meaning the issuer can pay you back before the maturity date, but you'd know when you purchase it if that is a possibility (it would be referred to as a *callable bond*).

So if you purchase a $1,000 municipal bond with a ten-year maturity, at 8%, that means you have loaned a municipality (i.e. a local government) $1,000 for ten years, and after ten years you would get your $1,000 back. In the meantime, you would be paid 8% interest, periodically, until the maturity date.

As an investment class, bonds historically have been less risky than the stock market because they are not as volatile; they are not subject to the swings of the stock market. On the other hand, like stocks, within the asset class there is a variety of risk levels. For bonds, the risks associated are evaluated by several rating agencies, the two most popular of which are Standard & Poor's and Moody's. The major risk that the rating agencies look at is the risk that the issuing party will not be able to repay your principal (this is called *default risk*). In other words, Standard & Poor's and Moody's are very much like Experian and Equifax; they tell potential lenders how good the credit of the party seeking the loan is.

If you buy only high quality bonds (U.S. government securities), you don't have to worry about your principal being repaid because such bonds are backed by the federal government. What you might have to worry about is the possibility that the value of your bonds might decrease if the interest rates rise. *Interest rate risk* refers to the reality that as interest rates rise, the value of bonds falls (and the converse is true). And the longer your bond has until its maturity, the greater the risk that the interest rate will rise.

You might be tempted to assume that if you wanted to buy a bond, you would go for a U.S. government security, such as a Treasury note, which could have a maturity of two years from the time you purchased it. However, that assumption is incorrect because the "safety" of that note comes with a price: a lower interest rate. If you want a higher rate, you'll have to get either a longer-term security, such as a Treasury bond (that matures in 10-30 years), or a lower-rated bond, which exposes you to a greater default risk. Just like when you are thinking about which stocks to purchase, bonds have several variables that determine how appropriate they are for your needs.

Types of Bonds

There are several different types of bonds, offering a variety of interest rates and a variety of maturities. The bonds that are likely to be in your portfolio are:

- Corporate bonds
  As the name says, these bonds are loans made to corporations. These bonds tend to have high yields and they are fully taxable. They are available in denominations of $1,000, and you usually are required to purchase at least five at a time.

- U.S. government securities
  As I explained earlier, these bonds are considered safe investments, because they are backed by the federal government. However, with that safety comes low interest and a tax at the state level.

- Municipal bonds
  Municipal bonds are issued by local governments and municipalities. They pay less interest than taxable bonds do, but they are exempt from federal tax and the tax of the state they are from (so buying your own state's bonds is a good idea).

Mutual Funds

A mutual fund is an investment with built-in diversification. We have all heard the old warning: "Don't put all your eggs in one basket." A mutual fund is composed of a variety of stocks or bonds, thereby minimizing the risks associated with any one particular stock or bond. Each mutual fund has an *objective*, such as growth and/or value, and you want purchase shares in the ones that have the same investment objective that you have.

There are probably dozens of funds that are appropriate for you; your planner will help you narrow them down by determining where your interests lie. For example, is your priority to get the highest returns possible (probable?), or do you have strong feelings that dictate how you invest, such as not wanting to invest in tobacco companies. You should be able to explain all of your investments to your children, and you should be proud of the decisions you make. I suggest educating yourself, thinking about your personal values, and choosing wisely.

Let me explain a mutual fund by demonstrating the difference between an individual stock and a mutual fund. If you wanted to invest in oil, you could buy shares in one oil company, such as Exxon. Or, you could invest the same amount of money in a mutual fund that invests in oil companies. This means your money would be invested, along with that of many other investors, in Exxon, and perhaps Gulf, British Petroleum, Tenneco, and many other oil companies.

The difference between the investment in Exxon and the investment in the mutual fund is most obvious in the possible results. Let's say Exxon had a major oil spill. The value of your investment would fall as a consequence, and it would keep falling until Exxon stabilized the effects of that oil spill. Exxon could go out of business altogether because of the oil spill. Or not. In any event, you are in bad shape, particularly if you needed to sell your shares (i.e., you would lose money).

However, if you had bought shares in a mutual fund that invests in oil companies, what would be the likelihood that all of them would have an oil spill? What would be the probability of all of them going out of business? If Exxon went out of business, you would not be in bad shape because only a portion of the fund is dedicated to Exxon. In addition, one or more of the other companies are likely to benefit from Exxon's folding, and you could be that much better off.

Mutual funds are the ideal investment for individuals who do not have the time, energy, or discipline to follow individual stocks. Each fund has a manager who analyzes the individual stocks and makes certain that their combination is serving the needs of the investors.

The Vocabulary of Mutual Funds

In order to maximize your time with your financial planner, I suggest educating yourself about the various types of mutual funds and terminology used to describe them and their investments.

- *Capitalization*
  Mutual funds are often described by the size of the companies that comprise them. Capitalization (cap) is term that refers to the total value of a company's stock, and the gradations of capitalization are: large cap, mid cap, small cap, and micro cap. *Large cap* funds invest in companies with over five billion dollars in total value. *Mid cap* funds invest in companies with one billion to five billion dollars in total value. *Small cap* funds invest in companies with a total value of 200 million to one billion dollars. *Micro cap* funds invest in companies whose total value is under 200 million dollars.

- *Growth Funds*
  Growth funds are usually composed of smaller companies that are growing quickly. They typically invest money back into their companies. The reinvested funds allow the companies to grow at a faster pace.

- *Value Funds*
  Value funds invest in companies that are considered solid and stable, but undervalued. They pay high dividends, but there is the risk that the companies were not undervalued and their stock price will not rise as anticipated.

- *Sector Funds*
  Sector funds invest in the stocks of a particular industry, such as utilities or biotechnology. There is considerable risk with sector funds as all of the companies in the fund will move in the same direction. If the industry is doing well, the entire fund is likely to be doing well, but if the industry is in a slump, there could be huge losses in the fund.

- *Foreign Funds*
  The United States is just one player in the global economy. We are a big player with a considerable amount of economic power, but that doesn't mean that American investors should put all of their money back into our economy. In fact, investing in the economies of other countries is a necessary part of any well-diversified portfolio. It actually increases the diversification of your portfolio because foreign funds have a low correlation to most domestic asset classes. In other words, a foreign stock, for example, doesn't necessarily move

in tandem with a domestic stock from the same industry. Investing in international and emerging markets may entail additional risks such as currency fluctuation and political instability.

There are basically four kinds of foreign funds:

1. *Global Funds* invest in developing countries of the world, including the United States. They are considered to be the most conservative of the foreign funds because of their inclusive nature.

2. *International Funds* invest in developing countries of the world, and do not include the United States.

3. *Emerging Market Funds* invest in countries that are not yet fully developed, such as Mexico, China, Korea, and Brazil. Remember that every country that is considered developed was once an emerging market. In England in 1909, a mutual fund called the "Scottish Investment Trust" was established. Its objective was to invest in an emerging market country called The United States of America.

4. *Regional Funds* invest in specific regions of the world, such as the Pacific Rim region. Country Funds invest in just one country. Country funds are considered to be the most aggressive of the foreign funds, because all of your eggs are in one basket.

Which fund is best for you?

There are many sources available for personal research of mutual funds. One of the most common is an independent rater called MorningStar, who publishes the results of their research in various forms. MorningStar's reports, which can be found at your local library and on the Internet (www.morningstar.com), tell you much of what you need to know in order to make your investing decisions. Other commonly used resources for analyzing mutual funds are Value Line, Ibbotson, and Wilson Associates.

Just as with stocks and bonds, before you begin your research you must establish your own personal objectives. Once you know what you want, you will know what to look for when you research funds. When you have found a handful of funds that match your objective, your next step is to compare them and choose among them.

What to look for in a Mutual Fund

Perhaps the most important item on any report about a mutual fund or any fund's prospectus (the report from the mutual fund company that explains the fund's details and history) is the fund's objective. When you (and your financial planner) find several funds that match your investment objective, your next step is to examine the fund manager's style. Though your planner can easily do this by herself, I urge you to involve yourself in the process. Remember, it's your money, and you want to know as much as possible about where it is and what is happening to it.

When examining the fund manager's style, look for consistency in what the kind of manager s/he claims to be, and whether fund reflects the alleged philosophy. For instance, does the manager claim to be a large cap growth investor? If so, has the manager been consistent and has the fund remained a large cap growth fund? The reason the manager's consistency is important is that when you invest in a mutual fund, your choice is usually made according to your objectives. And if the fund manager's style is inconsistent, your asset allocation will become skewed.

The fund manager's background is also important and should be examined. How much experience does the person have and how successful has s/he been? How did s/he fare when the rest of the market was up or down?

And as for the fund itself, you should always know exactly what your fund invests in—what you have invested in. You want to make sure that the companies you have invested in are ones you believe in. You also want to make sure that you are minimizing your overlap if you own more than one mutual fund. The only way that you can make sure you don't have overlap is to look at the list (which is often very long) of companies included in your mutual funds (or ask your financial planner to do so). And once is not enough because fund managers buy and sell all the time. I suggest asking your financial planner to pay special attention to the changes in the composition of your funds and apprise you of changes that cause overlap in your portfolio.

Your Insurance Needs

CERTIFIED FINANCIAL PLANNER practitioners look at your entire financial landscape, including your insurance needs. Most of the various types of insurance products are based on the same principle: you pay for something you might not need, such as health insurance and disability insurance. But some are purchased primarily for a different reason: as an investment.

Who needs Insurance?

Well that depends on which insurance products you are referring to. The types you need will be contingent upon many factors in your life, such as: your employment status, your marital status, whether you have children or other dependents, whether you own real estate, and whatever other possessions you own. The types most people should consider are:

- Health insurance
- Disability insurance
- Property insurance
- Liability insurance
- Life insurance
- Annuities

Health Insurance

When Bill was twenty-eight years old, self-employed (a photographer), very successful, very happy, and very fit and athletic, he fell off a cliff. Yes, this is a true story; he actually fell off a cliff. After breaking almost every bone in his body, he eventually healed completely. That was three years, a body cast, several operations, physical therapy, and well-over a million dollars later. Bill sold everything he had and his parents liquidated their assets as well, including a vacation home in Colorado. Both Bill and his parents borrowed money from friends and relatives also. Bill had to move in with his parents until he healed enough to go back to work. He recently finished paying back everyone who loaned him money.

Bill now has disability insurance and health insurance.

Many Americans do not have adequate health insurance. Individuals who are not conventionally employed are a large percentage of those people. Unfortunately, quality healthcare is not a given, and can be very costly. And all too often, when it is up to the individual to obtain her own health insurance, she postpones the purchase in favor of paying a bill or investing the money for retirement. After all, the logic goes, if nothing happens, that money was wasted. But if it was in the market, it could actually make you more money. That is a risky thinking considering what could happen to anyone at anytime.

There are many health insurance companies offering the various forms of health insurance. My point here is to compel you to include adequate health insurance coverage for yourself and any children you have in your financial plan as of this moment. Your financial planner will review your options and help you decide which is best for you.

Disability Insurance

The reality remains that when you are in your 20's, 30's, and 40's, the probability that you will become disabled is far greater than the probability that you will die. And while your dependents will be greatly affected if you become disabled, the party most profoundly affected is *you*. Where will your income come from? How will your bills be paid? Who will take care of you? Any person, single or otherwise, with or without children, who is self-employed, should have disability coverage. Your financial planner will explain your options and help you decide which plan is most appropriate for you.

Property Insurance

If you own a home, purchase homeowner's insurance. If you rent, purchase renter's insurance. It's that simple. Again, you will be purchasing a policy you may never need. But if you were burglarized while uninsured, how would you replace your clothing, jewelry, appliances, furniture and computer? And if you live in an area with a history of severe weather conditions such as hurricanes or tornadoes, you know that all it takes is a couple of minutes to destroy an entire block of homes.

Purchase insurance, and make sure you get enough to include your jewelry and other items that may need a rider. And before you get that coverage, you will probably need to authenticate and appraise your belongings.

Liability Insurance

You purchase liability insurance in order to cover expenses relating to someone being injured in your home or on your property (or in other ways by you, such as in the case of libel and slander). This policy can be purchased along with your homeowner's policy (i.e., an *umbrella* policy).

Life Insurance

Though we all know that we will die someday, some of us choose to ignore that reality. If there is anyone in your life who relies on you to support them, what is going to happen when you die? Where will the money they need come from? Furthermore, where will the money for your funeral come from?

Life insurance is necessary for any individual who has dependents. If you are single and have no children and are not the caregiver of your parents or anyone else, you do not need life insurance. But the moment someone becomes for any reason dependent on you financially, you should arrange to provide for that same support when you die. Therefore, life insurance is not something you should postpone purchasing; no one knows when their time to die is going to arrive. My urgent advice about life insurance is to make sure you (or your planner) shop around, as there is quite a disparity in rates for similar policies from different companies *for the same proposed insured.*

The two main types of policies you will have to choose from are called *term* and *whole life* and term insurance is usually a better buy. It is pure life insurance and can be purchased at a fixed, guaranteed rate. Whole life (also called universal life or variable life) is different in that it is also has an investment element to it. And as soon as you hear that, you should be thinking of one word: *commission.* This is why most insurance agents will be eager to sell you a whole life policy. There are some cases that warrant whole life, such as when it is for the purposes of estate planning (more on that in Chapter Seven: Estate Planning), so do your homework and ask your planner as many questions as it takes for you to understand and feel comfortable with her suggestion of a whole life policy.

Annuities

Annuities are insurance products that are also investments. They are contracts between you and an insurance company. When you purchase one of these contracts, the insurance company promises you a series of payments. These payments either begin immediately or at a later date (called immediate annuities and deferred annuities).

There are two kinds of deferred annuities: *fixed annuities* and *variable annuities*. Both types are tax-deferred investments, meaning you can put any amount of money in and the growth of that money will not be taxed until you take it out. Because of the tax-deferral feature, Uncle Sam will not allow you to take money out of a tax-deferred investment until you reach the age of 59½ without incurring a 10% penalty. In addition, the annuity company will also penalize you for early withdrawal, which again is defined as before you reach 59_. That penalty is called a *surrender charge*, and the amount varies according to the annuity company and the amount of the annuity. And any amount withdrawn, at any time, is subject to income tax. For these reason, annuities are used mostly for retirement planning (see Chapter Four).

There are two types of Annuities: fixed and variable. As the name suggests, fixed annuities offer a fixed rate of return. For example, let's say you wanted to purchase a fixed annuity at 6%. An investment of $20,000 would earn 6% for a period of time designated in advance by the annuity company. You would not be required to pay taxes on the 6% growth until you took the money out. At the end of the designated time period, the 6% rate could then be adjusted down or up.

Variable annuities are tax-deferred investments that offer investment options or sub-accounts. Variable annuities have the same IRS penalty as fixed annuities. They also have the same surrender charges if you withdraw funds prior to age 59½.

I prefer variable annuities because of the flexibility and diversity they offer. You can transfer into and out of the various fund sub-accounts at your discretion. And since such transfer is possible, as your investments vary, so does your rate of return.

Taking Control of Your Financial Passages

Regardless of your future plans, you will need to be acquainted (at the very least) with these major investment and planning issues. It's time for women—even married ones (especially married ones)—to learn about their money and the things that affect it. Before we go on to discuss the financial implications of relationships, let me leave you with some tips on taking responsibility for your financial life.

- Get organized

  Before you go to your financial planner, gather current statements from all accounts, and if you don't have a filing system, create one.

- Learn about the your tax situation and what affects it

  What is your tax bracket? Do you know what you can do to minimize your taxes? Do you know what upcoming events in your life might affect your tax situation?

- Choose your investments based on your values and beliefs

  There is a higher risk and a lower risk alternative to many investments. If there is something specific you are interested in participating in, tell your planner. If it is important to you to invest according to your beliefs and values, you may be somewhat restricted, but you will be happier in the long run.

- Know your investments

  If you haven't read all of the information regarding your accounts, do so as soon as possible. And get to know every investment and insurance policy you purchase. Your knowledge of your investments is both empowering and protective. The more you know about your finances, the fewer surprises you are likely to have and the better you will be able to anticipate and handle potential problems in advance.

Chapter Two

Couplehood and Parenthood

By Barbara Culver, CFP™

Jesse is a highly educated, successful entrepreneur in her late thirties. She has never married and she didn't think she would ever have children. Until recently. A year ago she met Mark, whom she instantly liked. He too is a successful entrepreneur who has never married. They recently decided to get married, and both of them are very excited and have no doubts about their love for each other. But they do have doubts—about how their finances are going to work.

Right now, Jesse and Mark live together and split all of their household expenses 50/50. They both make about the same amount of money, so all seems fair. But their recent concern is over what will happen when they marry. Will they co-mingle their funds, maintain separate accounts, or both?

They also wonder what will happen when Jesse has children. How are the finances going to work then? And if Jesse stops working, that means that Mark is responsible for 100% of the expenses of three people, plus saving for education and retirement! That worries both Jesse and Mark. In fact, all of these details worry them so much that they have postponed their wedding date because their heated discussions have become more frequent and worrisome.

The above scenario was rare forty years ago, but it is commonplace today. Many of the implications of conventional marriage are being scrutinized and found to be incompatible with the lifestyles of couples all over America. In fact, there are over four million opposite-sex couples living together in the United States. Many of those couples believe that living together solves the problems they have with the institution and ramifications of marriage. For example, the major disadvantage of marrying for successful working people like Jesse and Mark, is that they will pay more taxes when they marry than they would if they didn't (although that may change very soon).

But other than the marriage tax penalty, the fact is that there are few benefits to living together as opposed to marrying. (This does not apply to same-sex couples, who cannot legally marry, and individuals who are opposed to the institution of marriage and have no desire to have their relationship validated by the state.) For opposite-sex couples, cohabitation actually *creates* the potential for problems if you combine your finances, because the laws regarding non-married couples are not uniform and an agreement you have with your partner might not be enforceable.

As of 2001, thirteen states and the District of Columbia legally recognize the common-law marriage. This means that if a *man and a woman* live together as husband and wife for a specified number of years (check your statutes) they are considered married under common law. But regardless of your marital status, you have many of the same issues every other couple has.

Couplehood is a financial passage that should not be underestimated. Typically, the older you are, the more complicated your financial life becomes. If you have a partner now or if you have ever been married, think of when you first began sharing your life. When you are the only person you are thinking about and providing for, your financial life is relatively straightforward. Once another person becomes involved (and then maybe children), the details double (and triple . . .) and there are new concerns.

Before you decide to get married or cohabitate, the most important thing you can do is talk to your significant other about your thoughts and feelings about money. If you have this financial summit before you are married or move in together, and you decide how your finances are going to be handled ahead of time, you are less likely to become one of the many couples whose break-up was caused by disagreements over money.

The reality is that one-half of first marriages end in divorce, and of those divorces, the average length of the marriage is well under ten years. Many of those divorces will be of the ugly variety. And the most important issue in almost every one of them will be money. With that said, let's talk about the two words responsible for more anxiety than the idea of marriage or divorce . . .

Prenuptial Agreement

Marriage is a high-risk occupation. And for the woman who becomes the caregiver in the family unit, the financial risk is much greater. We are often warned to get life insurance to protect us in case of the death of a spouse, and disability insurance to protect us in case of a disabling illness or accident, and health insurance to make sure we are covered for the cost of doctors and hospitals. But for women, one of life's greatest financial risks is marriage, yet we are not encouraged to take steps to protect us from that risk.

If you are one of the many women who have a visceral reaction to the mere whisper of the words "prenuptial agreement," I suggest substituting the words "statement of intent," for now. And if you are still averse to the idea of considering a prenuptial agreement of some sort, imagine if, two months after you married, your husband decided to purchase a Ferrari with the money you both were saving for the renovation of your house and/or your children's educations. Even if most of that money was his, how would that make you feel?

If you are a woman who does not want to sign a prenuptial agreement because you consider it tantamount to preparation for divorce, you need to look at the reality of marriage in America. Ask any divorced woman and I promise you that when she got married she felt exactly the way you do: that she was certain that she had found the man she was supposed to spend the rest of her life with, that she trusted him implicitly, and that she could not imagine ever wanting to hurt him. She was equally sure that he would never intentionally harm her in any way.

What happened between then and the divorce? Could it happen to you? The statistics say you have a 50/50 chance. Knowing that, why would you proceed without first doing everything you can to protect yourself?

Prenuptial agreements are no longer exclusively for the super-wealthy. Over 5% of couples are choosing to agree in advance not only to how their assets will be divided if they divorce, but what will occur while they are married. Many prenups include specifications as to: who will pay the bills, where the couple will live, how often they will have sex, and even how they will drive. The scope of the prenuptial agreement has changed and many now approach the document as the opportunity to explain any and every thing they believe they need to make their marriage successful. In other words, many prenups in the third millennium are about marriage *preservation*.

Unmarried couples who live together often draw up a *living together agreement*, which describes, among other things, how the finances will be handled, how property will be owned and even monthly budgets. Remember that some states do not recognize such agreements, so if you are cohabitating you need to investigate whether the laws in your state have any provisions that explain how your break-up would be handled financially.

Marriage preservation is the angle I take regarding the maligned prenuptial agreement. My only goal when discussing prenups is fairness to all concerned. There are some situations that clearly warrant a prenuptial agreement, such as when one person has far more money (or debt) than the other, in the case of second or third marriages with children, when one person has family assets to protect, or when there is ownership in a business. And if you are currently in one of those relationships and a prenup is imminent, begin interviewing potential lawyers to represent you as soon as possible.

But just because you are not in one of the situations I listed as clearly warranting a prenuptial agreement, does not mean you don't need one. In fact, I recommend that every couple deal with their financial issues as soon as they are getting serious enough to consider marriage. And I recommend that every couple do it in writing. Few experiences turn sour as quickly as a surprise marriage proposal followed by a surprise request to sign a prenup. Such scenarios do not occur with couples who are honestly addressing all of the issues pertinent to couplehood.

My recommendations for couples beginning their lives together start with a simple, yet difficult task: Be completely honest about your financial situation. Your financial situation is perhaps one of the hardest topics to talk to anyone about. It makes you feel exposed and transparent. Many of your flaws and mistakes are revealed when you speak openly about your financial life. Ask any therapist who works with couples, and she will tell you that most people would rather talk about the details of their sex lives than the details of their financial lives.

The upside is that once you have told your significant other everything about your thoughts, feelings and habits regarding money, you will feel relieved, unburdened and even empowered. If someone leaves you after you opened your heart, mind and past for them to examine, you probably shouldn't have been with them to begin with.

When I say everything, I mean everything. Some of the worst situations I have seen began when the new couple tried to buy a house together and all kinds of surprises came out of the woodwork. Among them were enormous debts, poor payment histories, consistently maxed-out credit cards, bankruptcies and other aspects of the financial past that have a nasty habit of catching up to us at the most inopportune times.

Remember, when I talk about a prenuptial agreement, I am broadly referring to a statement of intent as a couple. Your planner might advise you each to get a lawyer to draw up a typical prenuptual document, stating who gets what in the event of your divorce. But in my opinion, that is not sufficient. I recommend, *at the very least*, that everyone construct a statement of intent for the purposes of clarifying expectations. And because relationships are organic and have a life of their own, I recommend that you periodically review your statement. And if you both agree that your intentions have changed, you may want to revise it.

Regardless of whether you choose to compose a legal document or an informal one, there are certain issues you ought to discuss to prevent future misunderstandings or worse.

- What kinds of items are okay to splurge on?
- What is the dollar definition of splurge?
- Who will take care of the family's finances? (Most women assume that responsibility.)
- What is your monthly budget?
- What is your savings plan? (And what exactly are you saving for? Tuition for a private college? A public college? What dollar amount are you shooting for?)
- What will your investment portfolio be composed of? (If you do not have the same risk tolerance, you need to reach a compromise on the types of investments you will purchase so you both are comfortable with the amount of risk your money is exposed to.)
- How will your property be owned? (There are tax implications and legal implications of the various types of ownership. Educate yourself so you make informed decisions. For example, if you buy a house together under *joint ownership with rights of survivorship* and one of you dies, the other automatically inherits the property. But if you own it as *tenants in common*, each of you is considered to own half of the home and if one of you dies, that person's share goes to whomever is named in their will.)

Your Relationship . . . with Money

In addition, during your financial summit, you should talk about your personal relationship with money. Money is something that has been a part of your life since you were born, and you have thoughts and feelings about it that you may not be aware of at this time. Before your relationship with your partner goes any further, you should attend to your relationship with money. After all, one guarantee I can make is that your money issues will be with you for the rest of your life. Gaining awareness and making peace with your feelings will help your relationship with your partner also.

The study of the psychology of money has been growing in popularity since the mid-1990's and, as a culture, America is finally admitting that our parents' relationship to money is largely responsible for how we feel about money as adults. Just like with sexuality, religion and language, we get much of our information about money from our family environments while we are growing up. I'm sure you've heard the phrase "children are like sponges." Remember that your propensity to absorb everything around you as a child included absorbing your parents' behavior regarding money.

There are entire books devoted to defining different money personalities. The following is a list of the basic things you need to know about yourself and your partner in order to thoroughly and responsibly begin your combined financial life. When you contemplate the questions below, don't judge yourself. Embrace whatever it is you have discovered about yourself, and whether you consider it negative or positive, think about why. If you have never examined your relationship to money, you'll find these questions to be quite revealing.

• *Are you a spender or a saver?*
Every person's childhood is unique. And although many adults choose to deny it, adults are continually making choices about what they will do and what will affect them. In other words, once you are an adult, blaming your parents for your financial situation is usually thinly-veiled rationalization. If you spend too much, it is because you are *choosing* to spend too much (or choosing to not keep track of your finances so you aren't even aware that you are over-spending).

Remember that there is no wrong or bad answer. Being a spender is not a bad thing; it depends on how much of a spender you are. And being a saver can be a curse. I know plenty of savers who are so stingy that they deprive themselves of basic things that are well within their standard of living. They secretly feel like they don't deserve even basic necessities, and that manifests in their tightfistedness (they usually call it "frugality"). In my opinion, a healthy spender who occasionally splurges on herself (within reason) is far better off.

• *Do you have difficulty sharing?*
Whether it is a slice of pizza or money, when it comes to something that you believe is *yours*, are you loath to share it? Does your skin crawl when you are asked to share? Do you find yourself specifying that things are "mine"?

• *Do you have difficulty spending on yourself?*
Do you find it easy to plunk down $350 for a cashmere sweater for your significant other, yet you shop for yourself at outlet malls an hour away?

• *Are you resentful of people who have more money than you?*
There are always going to be millions of people who have more things and more money than you. Does that bother you? Do you feel like you have been cheated? Do you wish you were, say, Ivana Trump, or some other high-powered, ultra-wealthy woman?

• *Do you feel like you are adequately compensated*
 for your work (I call it salary self-esteem)?
If you do not, do you address the topic or do you just smolder with anger because you think you should be making more money?

Before You Make Any Life-Altering Decisions . . .

Be honest with yourself about these questions and then, before you cohabitate with someone or accept a marriage proposal, ask your significant other to contemplate the questions, as well. Share your findings with the goal of attaining better understanding of each other. Again, the goal is not to judge.

After you have shared your findings, try to anticipate whether you are going to be able to live with your love mate. Anyone can fake compatibility for a short time. And many people appear to be compatible over the short term, particularly if they haven't had deep discussions about money.

Regardless of what happens during your unique conversations about money, there is one thing that you can count on: you are going to have to compromise in order to make your relationship work over the long term. This is especially true if your significant other's money psychology is very different from yours. Remember that adults are hard to change, and you don't want to enter a relationship with the hope of changing the other person. Such a plan is sure to fail miserably. Instead, work toward understanding the other person and finding a way to meet in the middle of the issues that you are separated most on.

- Maintain at least one bank account that is in your name only. Every woman should have money that is clearly hers and that she can spend any way she chooses. Also maintain at least one credit card in your name.
- Set up a joint account for household and other joint expenses (such as entertaining and traveling). Your contributions should be proportionate to your income (so if he makes twice as much as you, he should contribute twice as much). You might also want to set up a joint account for your children's educations.

And Then There Were Three

Anyone who has children will tell you that the moment they had their first child, their lives changed completely. One of the things that change when you have children is your financial priorities. For instance, if you didn't purchase life insurance when you got married, you certainly will now. And if you haven't already begun saving for tuition, when you give birth for the first time you will surely be thinking about it.

Tuition for what, you ask? Good question. I suggest that part of your prenuptial discussions are about your thoughts on the schooling of your future children. Some people feel very strongly about public schools; they wouldn't think of sending their children to private schools when their tax dollars are going toward some perfectly good schools. Other people feel strongly about sending their children to parochial schools. And then there are the people who want their children to go to school at the private school they themselves attended.

Whatever the case may be, you should be well aware of the future schooling expenses of your children before you even have them. After all, you want to know as much as possible about how much you are going to have to save so you can create a plan to meet your require-ments. Because tuition for most schools grows about two points *above* the inflation rate, you are going to need to create and stick to a plan if you desire to finance your child's education.

As with investing for other goals, the investments your planner suggests will depend on your tolerance for risk and the amount of time you have before you need the tuition. And as with other goals, there will be tax considerations and ownership considerations (e.g., education funds should be in your name, not your child's, as an asset in your child's name might hamper her eligibility for financial aid).

Common investments for parents who begin saving when their children are very young and who are concerned with the safety of their principal are: U.S. government securities, municipal bonds and CDs. Stocks and mutual funds, as always, present more risk but also greater potential for growth. Remember that the stock market has historically outperformed the other asset classes over the long term, so if you start saving early, the odds are in your favor that the stock market will be the better investment for your children's education funds.

The Next Step: Educate Your Children About Money

You are continually *passively* educating your children about personal finance. They watch what you do, they listen to what you say, and, as we all know, they have a keen awareness of inconsistencies and hypocrisy ("Do as I say, not as I do"). Your first step in educating your children is to develop an awareness of the messages you are sending with your actions.

When you tell them they don't *need* designer footwear, yet you are rarely seen in public without a little monogrammed horse on your shirt, you are setting yourself up for a problem. If you are fortunate enough that the problem surfaces immediately, you can do some damage control. But after years of double standards and inconsistencies between what you say and what you do, your children are likely to grow up not knowing the value of money *and* not trusting what you say.

Besides teaching your children about finance, the other advantage to paying careful attention to the messages you send is that you will probably save money. Why? Because you will be so cognizant of everything you purchase, and, like your children, you will question your decisions.

In addition to passively teaching your children about money, you also must actively teach them. And unlike sex (the other taboo topic), money is a topic that you can teach them about along with other fundamentals you teach them when they are toddlers.

According to a survey by John Nuveen & Co., in the year 2000 almost 50% of children in the United States said their parents never taught them the basics of money. If you are one of the many women whose parents taught her little or nothing about personal finance, I'm sure you have often thought about the negative affects of your financial illiteracy as a young person and all of the mistakes you made and opportunities you missed. You may even have blamed your parents for your mistakes. As a parent, you now have an opportunity to stop another generation of financial illiterates from developing.

The first step in teaching your children about personal finance is to let them know that it is okay to talk about it. Money should not be a taboo subject. Talk about your family's financial situation (within reason) in front of your children so they learn about salaries, taxes, banking, interest, borrowing, credit cards and investing (just don't *fight* about it in front of them). Talk about the consequences of spending, overspending and saving at a young age. Take them shopping for groceries and clothing and let them know how much things cost. Encourage them to comparison shop.

Fortunately, children are surrounded with opportunities to use numbers, and from early on they play games involving money. While that's a great introduction, I suggest giving them exposure to real money so they learn to identify it and relate it to consumer goods.

Explain to them that mommy and daddy work for money, and because of that work and that money, they can buy food, clothing and toys for their children. Help them to see the connections between money and their lives. I even believe in starting at a very young age (when they are comfortable walking and talking) with a weekly chores-for-pay system.

My only caveat is that chores are *not* things they should be doing as responsible individuals to keep their environment tidy and their bodies clean. In other words, no child should get paid for cleaning a room they have made a mess of. In addition, I believe every capable child should learn how to wash dishes, do laundry, use a broom and clean up a spill. This is especially necessary for boys, as their toys do not ordinarily teach such skills.

You don't want your children to grow up thinking that they will get paid for taking care of themselves or for doing well in school (they'll miss the real reasons: self-esteem and responsibility). Chores, then, are activities beyond those necessary for everyday living. Chores are things such as helping mommy and daddy clean out the garage or the basement, mopping the kitchen floor, or washing a car. I also suggest involving them in making the list for grocery shopping. This will help them figure out how much food (and money) their family consumes each week.

Explain to your children that they can save their money or spend it. Saving might not be as much fun as spending, but once you show them that they can purchase the toy or the jeans they want with their own money, they might see the value of saving. Be consistent with their allowance, discuss what they would like to do with their money, and then help them make a budget that allows for purchases or activities they desire.

The goal is not to give them money and watch them flounder and squander it all—it's to give them the information and tools necessary for them to succeed if they are disciplined and prudent. When they falter, give them emotional support, but try not to bail them out every time. Instead, help them understand what their mistakes were so they can learn from them and not repeat them in the future.

By the time they reach their teens, they should get a job outside of the home and immediately begin saving for a car, for college, or for their first home. If possible, match their savings, dollar for dollar. If they understand the idea of compounding and the time value of money by then, they'll surely be excited about the idea of a matching plan. This is also a good opportunity to teach them the difference when investing for short-term goals versus long-term goals.

Many mutual fund companies and even banks have products and programs geared toward children and young adults. The programs include camp-like sessions that teach personal finance through games, contests and role playing, and the products include investment accounts that you and their other relatives can add to as gifts on birthdays and other special occasions. Giving your children increasing responsibility for their financial lives as they get older empowers them. It gives them an edge that goes far beyond money. It builds their self-esteem and provides them with real-life skills that are vital to their success as adults.

Regarding credit cards, I suggest beginning with the debit variety, where your child secures the card with their own, saved money. (If you use your money to secure the account, your child will have less incentive to use it responsibly.) Once that card is used responsibly for six months, think about adding some money to it or getting them a credit card with a low limit.

Finally, let your children make their own mistakes. If they spend their allowance in one trip to the grocery store or the mall, and then they don't have money for the movie they planned to see with friends, that missed movie will stick in their minds for a long time. They will think twice the next time they want to spend all of their money.

> *From the lessons offered through the tapestry of time,*
> *we sift courage, love, integrity, wisdom and passion.*
> *Unshackled, we accept the challenge to create*
> *an inspiring future. With or without children,*
> *we are inseparable parts of the human experience,*
> *sharing a branch on the tree of life.*
> —Author Unknown

Chapter Three

Planning for Special Needs Children

By Roberta Welsh, CFP™

When my fifth child, Mary, was four years old, I tried to teach her how to identify herself in case she ever got lost. I told her we were going to play a game and that I was going to pretend to be a friendly police officer who wanted to help her. In my best, friendly policewoman voice, I asked her, "What is your name, little girl?" "Four," she replied. I smiled and corrected her, "Your name is Mary."

We played this game for several months, and each time she answered my query the same way. "Four." If she was teasing me, it was going on too long.

I became concerned. Upon reflection, I realized that her response to my simple question was not the only thing that was a bit off. Mary's physical development was slow, as well. And she was not learning to speak as quickly and as well as I thought she should. Relying on my mother's intuition, honed by raising four other children, I made an appointment with a child neurologist.

The neurologist administered a battery of tests over an entire day, and at the end of that day he invited Mary's father and me into his office. The doctor said the words that no parent wants to hear.

"Your daughter is mentally retarded." (No one used the

term "mentally challenged" in the 1970s.) "I think she can be educable, but I don't have a crystal ball. I suggest you put her into a pre-school so that she can begin the socialization process, as well as the education process."

Parenting a child with special needs creates a financial passage that can be devastating. Because it isn't the kind of situation you are likely to be prepared for, when it happens, many parents find themselves navigating a new emotional and financial landscape without a map. My intention with this chapter is to provide at least the most important landmarks on that map, with the caveat that this area is full of technical information and warrants the guidance of an expert.

The Landscape

Parents of children with special needs worry about all of the things other parents worry about, such as the health, socialization and education of their child. But the disability of the child creates a different environment and a host of different issues, for both parent and child. For instance, every time I visited a doctor's office or an emergency room with Mary, I was asked:

- "How long was your pregnancy?"
- "Could you have miscounted?"
- "Was your pregnancy normal?"
- "Was there anything unusual about your pregnancy?"
- "Was it the same as the previous four pregnancies?"
- "Did you fall during your pregnancy?"
- "Was the delivery normal?"
- "Were forceps used?"

Every time I heard these questions, I wondered if I had done something wrong. I felt guilty.

Then there are the many concerns parents have about their child's socialization. When Mary was first placed in a special education program, the "little school bus" would come to pick her up. The neighborhood children would stare at Mary as she boarded the bus. So did the children at her school. They noticed that she was different from them, and we all know that different is bad when you are in grammar school. My husband and I wondered how Mary felt about the hurtful comments, the smirks and the stares. We wondered if she was as angry as we were.

And if all of that wasn't enough, we wondered about the possibilities for her employment. Most young people get some kind of part-time job while they are in high school and they begin their journey to financial independence from their parents. But that destination wouldn't be possible for Mary.

When she was 16, she had a part-time job at a local grocery store. Her job was to bag the groceries, load them into a cart, walk the cart to the customer's car and load the grocery bags into the car. She was a conscientious and dependable worker and we were conscientious and dependable chauffeurs. As a part-time employee, Mary was not entitled to health insurance benefits or any other perks. We began to question what would happen to her health insurance when she was no longer eligible under our policy.

We wondered how we were going to be able to help her live as independent a life as she was able to live when she grew up. We began to research the laws and the possibilities for our daughter, and we were astounded by what we found. As of this writing, at the beginning of the year 2001, this is situation that children with disabilities and their parents have to contend with.

Health Insurance

Group health insurance policies usually allow coverage for dependents after the age of 18 *if they are students.* In most cases, this covers college-age children, and it can also cover those in special education in high school. Federal law allows those with developmental disabilities to remain in high school until age 22.

Once disabled people are out of school, they often can work part-time, but employer-sponsored health insurance programs usually do not cover them. So what can be done? The solution for many parents may lie in our nation's Social Security system.

Social Security

The Social Security system offers both financial help and medical help, through two different programs. When I describe the system in my seminars, I often begin by talking about something adults are familiar with: the retirement system. We all know that Social Security is deducted from our paychecks throughout our working years. The ideal is that at age 62 to 65, when we start getting monthly Social Security income, that income will be enough to support us. Of course, in today's dollars, the Social Security retirement amount is considered supplemental to our income needs.

What many people do not know is that age is not the only way to qualify for the "bucket" of money known as Social Security; you can also qualify if you have a disability or if you are blind. For the disabled population, the income is referred to as Social Security Disability Income (SSDI). Another kind of Social Security support that is available is called Supplemental Security Income (SSI).

Social Security Disability Income (SSDI)

Retirees receive income from Social Security and health insurance through Medicare. Similarly, people with disabilities receive income from Social Security Disability and medical benefits from Medicare. In both cases, a Medicare supplement policy (i.e., Medigap) is needed. However, while the retiree's Medigap policy can be purchased for an average cost of $105 per month, the SSDI recipient's monthly amount is often twice as much. That cost is usually absorbed by the parent of the special needs individual.

The difference in Medigap premium is just one of many difficulties facing families with special needs dependents. The problems usually begin years before, with the eligibility requirements for SSDI.

The eligibility requirements for SSDI support are that the special needs applicant has been determined to be disabled and has accumulated "credits" in the Social Security system by participating in the workforce. The criteria for determining whether the applicant is technically disabled are:

> In order to be considered disabled, an individual must have a medically determinable physical or mental impairment which is expected to last or has lasted at least 12 continuous months or result in death and (1) if 18 or older prevents him/her from doing any substantial gainful activity or (2) if under 18 results in marked and severe functional limitations *(1999 SSI Annual Report).*

Regarding the accumulated credits in the Social Security system, the applicant cannot draw on their parent's work record until the parent is receiving benefits (i.e., the parent is retired or disabled). The amount of the benefit the individual receives can be as much as $1,400 per month and is based on what they have earned. The recipient's work record, combined with the current amount per month, is reviewed each month. This means *the benefit can change monthly.*

Once a special needs person is receiving SSDI, however, there are also requirements for *continued eligibility.* For instance, if they have not been working and they decide to try to re-enter the workforce, they cannot earn more than $530 per month for nine months during 60-month period. And the nine months do not have to be consecutive. Once the nine months have accumulated, the dependent is considered to be gainfully employed, and their SSDI is terminated.

Supplemental Security Income (SSI)

Supplemental Security Income is a program for people with low incomes and limited assets who are 65 or older, blind, or disabled. If a disabled individual does not have medical insurance at age 22 because of no longer being a student, support can be obtained through Supplemental Security Income (SSI), which offers Medicaid.

Now, we've all heard of the stringent requirements of the Medicaid system, such as the asset (or *resource*) test and the income test. Currently, the special needs person may have no more than $2,000 of assets in their name ($3,000 for couples, if they are both receiving SSI), and no more than $550 per month of unearned income (which does not include wages, net earnings from self-employment, royalties and other work-related income). There is also a limit for earned income (and a complicated definition with many exclusions), but it varies for each individual case. It is important to study the definitions of earned and unearned income, as they are used in the calculation of all benefits.

Before the age of 18, it is the *parents'* resources and income that are used for the thresholds for SSI. Inevitably, most children are not eligible. Therefore, children need to reach 18 in order to qualify for Social Security help, because it is at this age that the asset and income tests are based on the *child's* assets and income. Age 18 is the critical age at which to apply to the Social Security system.

One exception to this is the child who qualifies for the Medicaid Waiver, referred to as *the waiver program.* Most often this program covers those children who ordinarily would be institutionalized if it weren't for their parents caring for them at home.

The SSI Benefit Amount

In 1999 the average SSI benefit was $369 per month, with payments varying with age, ranging from $450 for those under 18 to $293 for those 65 or older. This money is to be used for food, shelter and clothing. The maximum is $530 per person at this time, and that amount can be reduced each calendar month, depending on the individual's income and support.

Recipients receive the entire benefit if they live on their own or in a residential home. If they live on their own, the money is used for rent and living expenses. If they live in a residential home, they will use the SSI check to contribute to the cost of the home, including the monthly mortgage and the utility bills. If they live with their parents, however, the benefit *is reduced by about one-third* to account for the benefit they receive from living in the parents' house.

The Application Process

The actual application process for SSI/Medicaid is an obstacle of sorts in that it can be an emotionally wrenching for the parents. The parents fill out the application, which involves describing, in writing, all of the deficiencies their child has and how they manifest. That application is then sent to the office of the state's Disability Determination Service (DDS), where it is reviewed. A disability evaluation specialist and a doctor decide whether the child meets the Social Security Administration's definition of disability.

For me, the application process was truly grueling because for eight years I had concentrated on praising Mary's accomplishments. I wanted to be positive and contribute to her self-esteem. But now it was time to articulate all of the reasons why she was not able to take care of herself, why she probably could never have a full-time job and why she probably would always need assistance from the welfare program. I was forced to list all of the things I had been trying to forget, and all of the things my child was teased for and frustrated by.

Requirements of the Payee

Most parents are named *payee* and as such are required to complete a Payee Report each year. Essentially, Social Security wants to see how the money is being spent, and requires all pay stubs, bank statements and tax returns in order to support the requirement that the funds are being used for food, shelter and clothing. If any part of the SSI benefit is being saved, it must be reported, and it cannot exceed $2,000.

In the case of Mary, all was going along well with her SSI until age 24, when the Social Security office decided she was eligible for *SSDI* benefits because of her own part-time work record. She then began receiving SSDI checks and continued with Medicaid, until 1999, when her SSDI check was increased to over \$500/month. At this point she met the income threshold test and became ineligible for Medicaid.

As you can see, it is crucial to have a firm grasp of the system in order to best protect your child and not be surprised by changes in coverage. I recommend enlisting the aid of a CERTIFIED FINANCIAL PLANNER™ practitioner who specializes in planning for people with special needs—or another expert in this very specialized area—to help you understand the rules and the exceptions in order to prepare you for what lies ahead for you and your child. One of those exceptions is a designation known as the Adult Protective Child.

The Adult Protective Child

Al's daughter Cindy had been on SSI since the age of 18. Years later, when Al retired, Social Security notified Al that Cindy's SSI would change to SSDI. The rationale was this: Even though Cindy did not have enough earned credits for SSDI, her father did. And now that her dad was drawing on his benefits, hers would shift to the disability part of Social Security.

The income was similar, in fact Cindy received a little more that she was receiving under SSI each month, but there was a significant difference in her health care coverage. She was told that she was no longer eligible for Medicaid. Instead, she would be covered under Medicare, like retirees. So when Al applied for a Medigap policy for himself, he also had to get one for Cindy. That premium cost him \$250 per month for her, and \$103 per month for him.

By the time I met him, Al had been paying for this policy for six months, no questions asked. What he did not know at the time was that Cindy qualified as what is known as an Adult Protective Child and as such her coverage under Medicaid should have continued. (There is a Social Security rule that says that once there is a determination letter regarding disability between the ages of 18 and 22, the disabled person is considered an Adult Protective Child and can be eligible for Medicaid, providing they aren't gainfully employed.) Al approached the Social Security office about the discrepancy in coverage and was told that they had made a mistake, and that Cindy would be covered by Medicaid again. Since then, the local office has been able to red flag the computer so this shouldn't happen to anyone else in his area.

Planning for the Future

Most parents leave assets to their spouse as primary beneficiary and to their children equally as contingent beneficiaries. They do this through will, trust, or beneficiary designation on their insurance policies, IRAs, or retirement plans. In addition, many grandparents leave assets to their grandchildren, either by name or "per stirpes" (meaning to all of them equally). However, in the case of a child needing protection of their government benefits, any verbiage that makes a bequest causes a significant problem: the possibility of loss of SSI, Medicaid, SSDI and Medicare. When considering the disabled population, assets can be left in several different ways:

- To the dependent
- To a sibling (the morally-obligated gift)
- To a Special Needs Trust
- To a Community Trust (created especially for special needs participants)

Before you decide how you are going to leave your assets, you need to educate yourself about the consequences of your choices. Most of the errors in the financial planning of parents who have a child with a disability are made with the best intentions, but also with ignorance of some of the ramifications.

Leaving Assets to the Dependent who has a Disability

Recall that the dependent who is receiving SSI is subject to an assets test as well as an income test. They cannot have more than $2,000 in their name and they cannot have more than $550 per month in unearned income. So if the dependent with the disability inherits assets over the $2000 limit, they lose benefits, including Medicaid, until they have spent it all. If the dependent is not capable of managing the assets or income, a court-appointed financial guardian will need to be named.

> Judy is the daughter of a railroad retiree. There are few retirees who are allowed to name a joint beneficiary who is someone other than their spouse. In this case, the employee was able to name his daughter with a disability as the beneficiary of his railroad pension.
> The problem is that Judy will lose her SSI, as well as her

Medicaid when the pension begins because she will be receiving a stream of income. To remedy the situation her father was able to change the beneficiary from Judy to a Special Needs Community Trust. The manner in which the trust will pay for services will be discussed later.

Another example is the story of Jonathan, who was also a beneficiary of a railroad retiree . . .

Upon Jonathan's father's death, Jonathan inherited his pension. But when he began receiving a stream of income, he was disqualified from both SSI and Medicaid. The amount of the monthly check was not sufficient to pay for services or to enable him to obtain health insurance because of his disability.

Another way that at dependent can receive a sum of money is when they receive back pay from social security, get an inheritance, or are awarded a monetary amount due to a personal injury. If the amount is over $2,000, the disabled person's benefits will be discontinued until the money is "spent down" (to under $2,000).

A Solution to Inherited Money

In 1993 Medicaid passed a law, called OBRA '93, which states that the disabled person can give money to what is known as a Pooled Disability Trust. There are two types of Pooled Disability Trusts, the D4A Trust and the D4C Trust. The difference is that the D4C Trust is a charitable organization and the D4A Trust is not. The implication of that difference will become clear in a moment.

According to the Social Security Act, a disabled person can give their inheritance to the OBRA '93 Pooled Trust, which can in turn pay for services. The '93 law states that if a D4A Trust is used, any money left at the disabled person's death must be used to repay the state for the cost of services. But if a D4C Trust (a charitable organization) is used, any money left at the disabled person's death can remain in the charitable organization to benefit others, *and not necessarily repay the state.*

Leaving Assets to a Sibling (The Morally-Obligated Gift)

To protect entitlements, parents must avoid leaving assets to their disabled dependent. The parents also "disclaim" the dependent child by stating in their will or trust: "I leave my assets to my children equally except Mary." This is a heart-wrenching experience. But once the emotional hurdle is passed, it does offer an option: the opportunity for a sibling to act as payee.

While many a brother or sister would be happy to act as payee, financial guardian, or advocate, there are some issues that are worth mentioning:

- Acting as payee could place a burden on the sibling.
- The sibling might not always be geographically well situated.
- If the sibling does not live in the same area, acting as payee could be difficult.
- Acting as payee requires knowledge of the Social Security laws to ensure that the disbursement of funds would not be considered income to the beneficiary.
- Acting as payee requires awareness of any changes is the Social Security laws from year to year.
- The portion of the disabled dependent's inheritance could be subject to creditors.
- The portion of the disabled dependent's inheritance could be involved in divorce proceedings.
- If the sibling outlives the disabled beneficiary, the balance of the money could cause many family conflicts.
- The sibling could predecease the disabled dependent.

Someone needs to be the designated "payee" for the Social Security Income, and that person must file the Payee Report each year. The sibling should be prepared to do that and should also be prepared to act as an advocate for the beneficiary, as well as be in a position to communicate with social services. When assets are left to a sibling there is a great amount of trust and obligation implied. For example, there must be certainty that the sibling would not co-mingle the money, borrow any of the money, or subject the money to creditors or divorce proceedings.

Furthermore, with the transience of our society today, there is no promise of the sibling living nearby, which can result in costly communications with social services, the case manager and the residential counselor. Also, arranging a method of giving the dependent spending money can be difficult if the sibling is not nearby.

Leaving Assets to a Special Needs Trust
(a third party-funded trust)

Instead of disclaiming a dependent as beneficiary, the parent can leave any share of an inheritance to a Special Needs Trust for the benefit of the dependent child/adult. This trust contains special language that protects the dependent and the entitlements.

Monies in the trust cannot be used for food, shelter or clothing, nor can they provide an income stream. Funds can be used only to pay for services, and must be paid directly to the service provider. Examples of such services are:

Medical costs not covered by Medicaid, Medicare, or supplemental policies

- Routine dental care
- Eyeglasses or their repair
- Alcohol and drug abuse therapy
- Routine physicals and immunizations
- Day care
- Annual OB/GYN exams
- Optional health insurance premiums (dental insurance, Medigap policy, long term care insurance)
- Some medical equipment
- Vitamins

Entertainment
- Movies
- Video rental

Sports
- Special Olympics
- Bowling, ice skating, roller skating, skiing, baseball, basketball, swimming

Vacations
Travel to visit other family members
Traveling companion
Transportation

Household expenses
- Cable
- TV
- Telephone bill
- Cleaning
- Educational classes or programs

When the beneficiary dies, the balance of the assets in the Special Needs Trust can revert back to the family. The assets can also stay in the trust to benefit other individuals. The parent, or the third-party donor, has the choice.

Other Trust Options
Depending on the gross estate of the parents, another option would be to leave the money in a charitable remainder trust, so that the dependent can be financed through their lifetime, and the corpus would then go to a charitable organization (for more on charitable remainder trusts, see Chapter Eight: Philanthropy).

The parent can also create an irrevocable trust. The parent can be the trustee or can name the trustee, such as a family member, a corporate trustee, or both. A corporate trustee charges for acting as a trustee, and their fee is usually a percentage of the assets in the trust. Often the minimum amount of money in such a trust must be $250,000 to $500,000 to be of interest to a corporate trustee. In all probability, the corporate trustee will not act as payee for Social Security purposes, advocate for the beneficiary, or realize the reporting requirements necessary for Social Security and Medicaid.

Leaving Assets to a Community Trust (a Special Needs Trust)
Many states have created a master Special Needs Trust referred to as a Community Trust. The master trust reads as a Special Needs Trust with language that protects the dependent's government entitlements.

Ordinarily, the Community Trust is set up as a tax-exempt organization (a 501[c]3). A corporate trustee is often chosen and works with a board of advisors. The board typically consists of parents of children with disabilities and professionals who are especially interested in this population. Because it is a group effort, the administrative costs are lower than that of an individual trust. In addition, there is no need to have an individual Special Needs Trust drafted by an attorney since the master trust is already in place. One becomes a participant in the master trust by way of a joinder agreement, which available to anyone in the state.

The Community Trust is often the best choice for parents of children with disabilities for the following reasons:

- The Community Trust can act as payee.
- The Community Trust can act as an advocate.
- The Community Trust is often in the best position to communicate with both the beneficiary and the case manager or family member.
- The Community Trust would be able to keep up with the changes in the Social Security Codes while having the best interest of the beneficiary at heart.
- The Community Trust has the capacity to own a residence, either by inheriting the beneficiary's house through the will or by having the money to buy a house, and convert it to a group home.
- The Community Trust has already established a system to comply with the reporting requirements of Social Security and Medicaid.
- The Community Trust usually provides income tax reporting for the dependent.

Reporting
Regardless of whether a sibling, a corporate trustee, or a Community Trust trustee manages the assets for the dependent, Social Security, Medicare and Medicaid require diligent reporting. They need to know when a trust is funded and when checks are issued.

Funding the Special Needs Trust
Most parents do not have the liquid assets to fund the trust with assets during their lifetime or at their death, so the best possible way to fund the trust is often through life insurance. This allows the parents to divide their estate equally among the remaining beneficiaries while leaving a life insurance policy to the special needs child by way of the trust. The challenge today is the reality that no one knows how long the current government benefits will continue. And for many, there won't be enough housing and services to go around.

Consider the statistic that approximately 6% of the population is born with a disability and only about 2% can be served through government benefits. Many of us will need to finance housing, case management and transportation, to name just a few major costs. If you estimate the cost of services in today's dollars to be between $50,000 and $75,000 annually, a life insurance policy with a death benefit of $500,000 would not be excessive. In some states, there is a maximum amount allowed in a Special Needs Trust, so be sure to consult your financial planner about the amount and type of insurance you should purchase.

The kind of life insurance can vary, but all parties in this situation are usually best served by whole life/universal life insurance, or a "first to die" or "second to die" policy. It depends on the family situation. The best of all worlds is to insure the grandparents, especially if they can help the parents pay the premium.

Another critical planning issue is the ownership of such a policy. A $500,000 policy could push a couple's estate over the unified credit amount, which is $675,000 per person in the year 2001. Above $675,000, estate taxes are triggered. To avoid this, it would be wise to have the Special Needs Trust or a Community Trust own the policy as an irrevocable trust in order to remove the death benefit amount from the parents' estate or the grandparents' estate (see Chapter Seven for further explanation of Estate Planning).

The Family Mission Statement or Letter of Intent

The next most important aspect of planning for the beneficiary is the piece of communication between the parents and the caregiver known as the Family Mission Statement, or, Letter of Intent. Essentially, this document expresses your wishes with regard to your child in the event of your disability or death. Here are some things you should be thinking about if you have a child with a disability.

1. Have I planned for someone to serve as guardian, financial guardian, or Payee?
2. Have I planned for my child's final arrangements (e.g., burial place, cremation, religious service)?
3. Is my dependent with a disability capable of signing a living will or an advanced medical directive?
4. Have I set aside any funds for my child's financial security?
5. Is my wish for my child to live alone, with a roommate (same sex or other), or in a supervised living situation?
6. Is my will drafted to protect my child by name?
7. Do I have a Special Needs Trust to manage my child's resources?

8.   Have I met with relatives and friends to inform them of my written plan?
9.   If I have a written plan, have I reviewed it in the last year?

When you are composing your Letter of Intent, it should include details about the life of your dependent. The following is a list of some of the information you should gather for your written plan. Ask your planner what other details need to be included in your Letter of Intent, as it should be comprehensive.

- Information about the mother, father, and siblings.
- Date/place of birth of parents.
- Mother's maiden name.
- Information about the person with a disability.
  - › Date/place of birth
  - › Legal guardian
  - › Representative payee
  - › Power of attorney, medical directive, living will, will
  - › Final arrangements
  - › Medical history and care
    - » names of all health care practitioners, past and present. Include physicians, surgeons, dentists, nurses, eye doctors, and frequency of check-ups
    - » insurance, past and present
    - » diagnosis: speech, hearing, mobility, seizures, vision, functioning
    - » prescriptions, nursing needs, mental health, therapy, diagnostic testing, genetic testing, immunizations, diseases, allergies, other problems, procedures operations, hospitalization, birth control medication/devices, other medication
    - » medical equipment

Conclusion

As you can see, many unique issues are triggered when you have a child who has special needs. This specialized area can be very confusing, particularly for the parents who are experiencing a spectrum of new emotions and worries. For these reasons, it is imperative that you find a planner who is sympathetic and knowledgeable about your situation.

If we don't financially protect our children with disabilities, their

future will be uncertain and can be grim. Obtaining expert advice, educating yourself and keeping current with tax law are of paramount
importance. Give yourself the gift of peace of mind by knowing that you
have done everything you could to protect the future of your children.

Chapter Four

Career and Retirement

By Carter W. Leinster, CFP™

Women make 70 cents for every dollar men make.

Two thirds of single women over 65 have no income other than Social Security.

The income from Social Security for a woman is usually less than for a man.

Three out of every five women face old age without a husband.

Four out of five women die single.

Almost 75% of elderly people living below the poverty level are women.*

The most important financial investment for women should be their own financial independence.

The purpose of this chapter is not to dwell on discouraging statistics, but to compel you, through a review of reality, to prepare yourself for your passage to retirement. Most women are in the unfortunate position of having to work harder and longer than men to save the same amount of retirement money. Why?

1. The amount of most employer-sponsored retirement benefits, as well as the size of Social Security payments, depends on the level of income earned over many years of work. Therefore, if a woman has earned less than a man throughout her career, her retirement benefits will be less.

* The above statistics are based on information from the Select Committee on Aging, House of Representatives, September 1992.

2. Women, on the average, earn less than men. The lower your
    income is, the smaller the amount of discretionary funds you
    will have available to invest for retirement.
3. Women live longer than men. The average life expectancy of an
    American woman is seven years longer than that of the
    American man. In fact, most married women will live their last
    years as widows. And in many cases, their husband's illness prior
    to death will have consumed much of the couple's financial
    resources, leaving the widow in a detrimental financial position
    for her remaining years. *80% of widows now living in poverty were
    not poor prior to the death of their husbands* (Retirement
    Subcommittee of the Congressional Aging Committee).
4. Women tend to be in and out of the work force more than men.
    In most cases, it is still the woman in our culture who stays
    home or works part-time in order to care for children or elderly
    parents or parents-in-law.

    In most employer-sponsored retirement plans, the employee
    must be employed full-time for one year before being eligible to
    participate. Once participation begins, it often takes five years
    of employment to be *100% vested* in the plan (i.e., it often takes
    five years before 100% of the money in the employee's account
    belongs to her). Leaving prior to that time means that only the
    part of the account to which she has contributed belongs to her,
    and the rest remains in the plan to be reallocated to the
    accounts of the employees who continue to work there.

    Therefore, a woman who has to move in and out of the work
    force because of family responsibilities may never 100% vest in
    the retirement plans she participates in. Furthermore, without
    continued "years of service" a vested benefit could be quite
    small compared to the amount of earned income.
5. Retirement has traditionally been the responsibility of the hus-
    band, who has usually been the primary income earner in a mar-
    riage. My observation from my financial planning practice has
    been that even though many married women are now part of
    the work force, most retirement income planning is still tied to
    the husband's employment. The result is that the husband is
    assumed to be the decision-maker. This situation becomes espe-
    cially difficult for the wife if her husband becomes ill or unem-
    ployed, since she must take on a new responsibility that can be
    very stressful if she has no prior experience with it.

Fear of Becoming a Bag Lady

Many women are all-too familiar with the statistics I mentioned and the descriptions of the state of our gender. Because we know that information is true intellectually, experientially, or both, many of us fear becoming bag ladies. If you secretly have this fear, comfort yourself with the thought that you are not alone.

My concern is that given this state of affairs for women, combined with the fears we have, why do many of us find it so difficult to take control of planning for our financial future? I think I know why . . .

Procrastination

So many of us lead busy lives as we juggle the demands of family, job and community, that learning how to save and invest wisely seems to be an enormous endeavor. For many who have had little experience with financial planning, it seems that this new task is difficult and will take a long time. And when something seems so complicated and overwhelming, it's easy to discover lots of ways to avoid doing it.

Procrastination also results when you choose to continually put the needs of others before your own, which is a common trait among women. This is the most insidious type of procrastination because it is masked by what appears to be altruism. Keeping yourself busy helping others is a great excuse for not taking care of your own needs.

Fear of Making Mistakes

Some people would rather do nothing than risk making a mistake. Often this is because they do not want to appear ignorant about something they think they should know about. When you discover that there is so much you don't know—that you think you should know—you could become so paralyzed by your realization that you don't even know where to begin.

You might think that if you were to make a mistake you would reveal your ignorance to all, and you subsequently would suffer some kind of humiliation for not educating yourself sooner. But I guarantee you that even if that happens, it's better than never learning at all. Remember that it takes courage to admit you don't know something and to ask for help.

Thinking That it's Too Early to Prepare for Retirement

Women in their twenties and thirties often do not take advantage of the retirement plans available to them. They think they have plenty of time to prepare and that their priorities should be the high expenses of a home and children. But *the time value of money* teaches us that the money we earn in our twenties is the most powerful of all because it has the most time to grow—to compound. I'll demonstrate the significance of time a bit later.

These are just some of the reasons why women neglect their own retirement planning. However, regardless of how frightening, overwhelming, or complex the details of your retirement planning may seem to you now, they are far less terrifying than the alternatives. Reread the statistics at the beginning of the chapter the next time you think that retirement planning is not something you need to think about. The financial passage to retirement, unlike the other passages, is an issue that every woman should start to think about decades before it occurs.

My First Recommendation

My intention for this chapter is to explain the core issues involved in retirement planning for women. I will provide you with much of the basic information you need to understand in order for your financial advisor to be as helpful as possible to you. I urge you to empower yourself by using this chapter as an outline for your financial education. Your future financial independence depends on it.

Planning for Your Retirement

I know a handful of people who do not need any help preparing for their retirement. They are all financial planners. In my opinion, everyone else needs some help. The first step is to locate a financial advisor whom you like and trust. (Lois Carrier explained that process in Chapter One. If you are skipping around, be sure to read that chapter next.) The next step is to prepare for your meeting about your financial independence and your retirement.

The most important pieces of information you need to help your advisor *help you* most efficiently and effectively are the ones about the sources of your retirement income. Your future income will probably come from these three sources:

1.   Government (Social Security)
2.   Employer-sponsored retirement plans (yours and/or your spouse's)
3.   Personal savings and investments

Social Security

Social Security is gradually providing less security as a source of future income and here's why: As our population ages and our life expectancy increases, there are fewer and fewer workers paying into a system that is supporting more and more retirees. Moreover, for many retirees, a portion of their Social Security payments (up to 85%, depending on other income sources) has become taxable income. Finally, the annual increases in Social Security payments have changed from being close to the inflation rate to lower than the inflation rate.

Meanwhile, the age at which a full benefit is available is increasing. For individuals born before 1938, the "Normal Retirement Age" for full benefits is 65. For individuals born after 1938, the age to receive a full retirement benefit is slowly increasing to age 67. This means that for most workers today, it will be necessary to work past age 65 in order to get full Social Security benefits.

There are many complex rules concerning Social Security. For now, you should acquaint yourself with the basics:

- You become eligible for a retirement benefit when you have worked and paid Social Security taxes for 40 quarters. You will also be eligible to receive a spousal retirement income from Social Security if your spouse has paid Social Security taxes for at least 40 quarters of work.
- The amount of your Social Security retirement benefit depends on how many years you worked and what your income was during those years. The average of the highest 35 years of earnings is used to compute the benefit. If you did not work for some of those years, a "0 earnings" is counted into your total average earnings for each year you did not work.

  Therefore, a woman who was employed for only 20 of the 40 years prior to retirement would have a much lower average earnings than a woman who was employed each year, even if they made the same income during the years they both were working.
- The amount of the benefit also depends on when you begin to

take the payments. At the present time, for workers who
reached age 61 before the year 2000, the "Normal Retirement
Age" is 65 for a full benefit. If you decide to start receiving benefits at age 62, the benefit will be 20% less than the full benefit
amount. If you choose to wait until after age 65 to start receiving Social Security, the benefit is greater than the age 65
amount. For workers who reach age 62 in 2000 or later, the age
necessary to receive a full benefit is gradually increasing. If you
will reach age 62 after the year 2022, the age for full retirement
benefits will be 67.

- The Social Security payment to a *lower* paid worker is a greater
  percentage of the pre-retirement income of that worker than
  the percentage that the benefit represents of the pre-retirement
  income of the *higher* paid worker. For example, the worker who
  has worked for many years and who retires at age 65 with a pre-
  retirement annual income of $25,000 and is eligible for a full
  benefit will receive a monthly benefit today of about $850. This
  is about 41% of that worker's total monthly pre-retirement
  income. The worker who retires today with an income of
  $80,000 will receive a maximum monthly benefit of about
  $1,500. This is about 23% of that worker's pre-retirement
  monthly income. (It is important to remember that these
  amounts increase a little each year. The amounts noted are for
  the year 2001.)

- If you are married at the time that your husband begins receiving Social Security benefits, you are eligible to receive a benefit
  based on his account. If you are 65 when you begin receiving
  the spousal benefit, it will be 50% of your husband's amount. If
  you begin receiving your spousal benefit when you are 62, you
  will receive about 37.5% of your husband's benefit. (It is important to remember that as the age to qualify for a full benefit
  increases, the age to qualify for the larger spousal benefit
  increases as well.) If you are eligible for a benefit on your husband's account as well as your own from your working years,
  you will receive the higher of the two amounts. The earliest you
  can receive a retirement benefit, either on your account or on
  your spouse's, is age 62.

- If you are divorced from your husband at the time he is eligible
  to receive Social Security benefits, you can still receive a spousal
  retirement benefit if you were married to your ex-husband for
  at least 10 years *and* you have not remarried. If you have remar-

ried by the time benefits begin, you will receive a spousal retirement benefit based on the account of your current husband.

- If you are widowed before your husband's Social Security payments would have begun, you can receive a widow's benefit at age 60. If you are widowed after Social Security payments have begun, and you were receiving spousal benefits, you will continue to receive the higher of the two benefits: yours or your husband's, but not both.

- It is important for both you and your husband to check your Social Security accounts every 3-5 years. The Social Security Administration can provide you with a listing of the amounts of the income that were used each year to determine your Social Security taxes. It is important to be certain that each year you had an income is counted. You should also double check that the *amount* of income reported to the Social Security Administration for each of those years is accurate. The Social Security Administration can also provide you with an estimate of your future benefits. The form to request this estimate can be obtained from your local Social Security office, by calling 1-800-772-1213, or by going to their web site (www.ssa.gov).

Even with the continuing changes in Social Security payments, it seems likely that some form of Social Security will continue for at least a part of our population in the future. However, it is clear that you should not depend on Social Security as your main source of retirement income.

Notes on Self-Employment

Fact: Women-owned firms account for nearly forty percent of all businesses in the U.S. according to the National Foundation of Women Business Owners.

Fact: The Small Business Administration estimates that 9.1 million women-owned firms contribute more than 3.6 trillion dollars in sales and revenue to the U.S. economy annually.

One of the most difficult situations I encounter is with young, self-employed women. Many do not have adequate health insurance or disability insurance, and do not have any retirement savings. Many are not handling their taxes correctly (i.e., they are not making quarterly payments) and do not know which of their expenses are deductible.

Though self-employment has many advantages, one of the disadvantages is that you are forced to provide yourself with benefits that are automatically included with conventional employment. And when the purchase of health insurance and disability insurance is up to you, you just might take a risk and put it off because you'd rather keep the money.

Unfortunately, the same is true for retirement savings. Any self-employed person can open a SEP-IRA (a retirement savings account for self-employed individuals—more on that later). But when no one is going to match your contributions, and retirement is a long way off, it often seems less important or urgent to begin saving.

For the self-employed, probably the only thing worse than not having adequate insurance coverage or retirement savings, is not making timely quarterly tax payments. A benefit of conventional employment is that your taxes are taken out of your paycheck for you; you never see the money. Though many people complain about this reality, in my eyes it is one of the most favorable aspects of conventional employment.

Imagine this: You work at a conventional job and one day your employer says to you, "This year, rather than taking your tax money out of your paycheck, I'm going to leave that up to you." How many people, particularly those experiencing a financial crisis, might opt to *postpone* sending their taxes in? Would you? If so, you would of course *plan* to send them in as soon as the crisis was over. But what if the original crisis ended and a new one began? What if postponing your tax payment would allow you to purchase health insurance? Or what if the original crisis ended and you found a new, diamond-encrusted watch (it's just an example; insert your favorite pricey item) that you absolutely *had* to have, *and it was on sale*? What would you do then?

This is the quandary of the self-employed; they get to choose what they want to do. It only becomes a problem when they choose to not follow the rules, because shortly after a quarterly payment is due, another one is due. And if you haven't paid the first one on time, you get to pay interest and penalties in addition to the second one. It takes only one setback like this to put you on the path to financial ruin.

If you are self-employed, you need to be especially careful of your bookkeeping, your paperwork, your insurance needs and your taxes. Ask your financial planner to recommend a good accountant, as keeping up with the tax laws, particularly in the area of retirement planning for the self-employed, is a full-time job.

Employer-Sponsored Retirement Plans

This source of retirement income includes income originating from your spouse's employment as well as your own. As I discussed earlier, these benefits are often less for women than they are for men. Later in the chapter, I will describe the most common types of employer-sponsored retirement plans.

Personal Savings and Investments

What you choose to do with the money that you earn (after taxes) or receive as gifts is the part of your money that you have the most control over. And *because* you have the most control over it, it is the source of retirement income that requires the most attention and discipline. After all, you can easily choose to not put part of your paycheck into a retirement account. At that moment, you can always convince yourself that the money is better spent on whatever immediate need or desire you have. Rarely does putting an extra $2,000 or $5,000 away for 20 years look better than upgrading your car or buying a new couch, particularly when you need one.

How Much Do You Need?

The best way to plan what you need to save and invest for your retirement is to determine how much you will need at retirement in order to generate adequate income in the future. This number is the guide that tells you how much you need to save and invest between now and your retirement. Your planner will have a formula for calculating how much you will need, but you are going to have to be involved in order for the process to be most effective.

The first step for you is to determine how much of your current expenses will also be expenses when you retire. Many people use a formula that estimates your expenses, but I recommend dispensing with the formula in favor of determining exactly how much money you are spending in order to maintain the lifestyle you are accustomed to. This entails itemizing *all* of your expenses. For instance, food (including dining out and entertaining), clothing, transportation and utilities are all expenses today that you will also have when you retire. On the other hand, if your mortgage will be paid in full by the time you retire, you will not include it in your calculation. Don't forget that property taxes and insurance will continue each year, even after the mortgage payment ends.

This number that represents how many of today's dollars it takes to maintain your life in the way you are accustomed, is a number you should always know. This is not an exercise that is necessary only if you are planning for your retirement. *Every woman should be constantly aware of how much money that she, and others, are spending on her lifestyle.*

Again, in order for your planner to create the most effective plan, she needs to have the right numbers to work with. Regardless of how great your financial planner is and how much you trust her to do anything for you, I recommend doing this exercise yourself. You will learn a lot about yourself, particularly, *where all of your money has been going!*

I have provided Worksheet 1 to help you organize your income and expenses. Be sure to convert your monthly expenses to annual amounts. This worksheet can be used for you alone or for both you and your spouse or partner. Take the time necessary to be as thorough as possible.

Worksheet 1
Income and Expenses
Part 1: Income

MONTHLY   **ANNUALLY**

Total Earned Income
(This amount is your salary, commissions and self-employment income *after* all of your expenses; it is a net amount)

_____   _____

Dividends, interest and capital gains

_____   _____

Annuities, pensions and Social Security

_____   _____

Rental Income

_____   _____

Other

_____   _____

Total Income

_____   _____

Worksheet 1

Income and Expenses
Part 2: Expenses

(circle those you will have during retirement)

MONTHLY   **ANNUALLY**

Income Taxes-Federal and State (if applicable)
Check your return for amounts. Do not use the number on your pay stub, as the amount withheld may be more or less than the actual tax owed.)

_____   _____

Social Security Taxes

_____   _____

Payments to Retirement Plans and IRAs

_____   _____

Mortgage/Rent

_____   _____

Food (at home and away from home)

_____   _____

Medical Expenses (not reimbursed by insurance)

_____ _____

Medical Insurance Premiums

_____ _____

Utilities

_____ _____

Telephone/Cable

_____ _____

Car Payment

_____ _____

Car-gas and parking

_____ _____

Car-maintenance, licenses

_____ _____

Clothing

_____ _____

Childcare

_____ _____

Children-classes and camps

_____   _____

Tuition or Education Expenses

_____   _____

Insurance Premiums (home and auto)

_____   _____

Insurance Premiums (life and disability)

_____   _____

Maintenance of Home

_____   _____

Property Taxes

_____   _____

Personal Care (haircuts, cosmetics, etc.)

_____   _____

Hobbies

_____   _____

Entertainment/Club Memberships

_____   _____

Vacations and Weekend Trips

_____   _____

Pet Expenses

_____   _____

Professional Fees/Memberships

_____   _____

Subscriptions/Books

_____   _____

Gifts and Donations

_____   _____

Holiday Expenses

_____   _____

Loans, Credit Card Payments
(Try not to double count with other categories.
Either put credit card payments here or allocate
them to other specific expense categories—not both.)

_____   _____

Miscellaneous

_____   _____

Total Expenses

_____   _____

TOTAL INCOME   _____

(minus) TOTAL EXPENSES   _____

TOTAL AVAILABLE   _____
FOR SAVINGS/
INVESTMENTS

Surprised?

I have yet to see anyone go through her expenses from prior years and *not* get angry with some of the choices she made (most are noted under "miscellaneous"). Most women will claim they weren't consciously choosing, say, a new watch over putting money away for retirement. But the fact is that each time you spend money on something, you are choosing to not put that money elsewhere. Let's keep the past in the past, yet also keep it in mind and learn from it. Make your past your friend rather than your foe.

How Much *Will* You Need?

Your next step is to go through your annual expense list and circle the items that are likely to *always* be expenses, whether you are retired or not. You probably will *not* circle Social Security taxes, payments to retirement plans, mortgage payments (if you expect to pay it off before you retire or shortly thereafter), or children's expenses. Be sure that property taxes and home maintenance expenses (including an amount to be reserved for major repairs) are circled as continuing expenses. Also be certain that you include an ongoing expense for car payments or a reserve amount to buy a car when needed. This is an important item that is sometimes overlooked if you are not making a car payment at the time you are working on this list.

Pay special attention to medical insurance premiums. If you do not pay one today because you are included in a group health plan where the employer pays the premium for you, ask what the premium is and include it in your expenses. It is very likely that you will have to pay a health insurance premium after you retire.

Once you have circled all continuing items, add them together. This is the amount of money you would need *today* if you were retired.

How To Create the Retirement Income You Need

The calculation for how much you will need to accumulate by the day you retire will involve subtracting the total you will *have* from the total you will *need*. Bring your lists and calculations to your planner, along with the current statements from whatever retirement accounts you have. Those figures, along with your Social Security information (call for an estimate of your benefit), will be used to calculate how much you will *have*.

The Total You Will Need (your planner will calculate this)

minus

The Total You Will Have (based on how much you have now)

The Total You Need to Create

If you completed Worksheet 1, part 2 and the result was that you barely cover all of your expenses, don't despair. No one gets to 40 years old without any retirement savings intentionally; they do it because they weren't educated about what they could have done. Let's look at some factors that will put you on your journey to making your comfortable retirement a reality.

1. The Time Value of Money

Perhaps you've heard the phrase, "the magic of compound interest." In my experience, this phenomenon is best grasped by examining a simple chart.

The Result of Investing $2,000/year with an Annual **8%** Return

Years	Total	Will Grow To
5	$10,00	$ 12,672
10	20,000	31,291
15	30,000	58,649
20	40,000	98,846
25	50,000	157,909
30	60,000	244,692
35	70,000	372,204
40	80,000	559,562

Note that as the investment has more time to grow, the value increases more rapidly. This is why it is so important to begin the process of regular long-term investing early. Doing so allows the impact of compound interest to make the maximum impact on your journey to your retirement income goal. This chart illustrates the reality that time is your most powerful ally for retirement saving.

2. Small Amounts Make a Difference

Too often, I hear a client say, "Yes, I understand about the time value of money, but the amount I am able to invest now is so small that it wouldn't make a difference. I'll wait until I can save more before I start." But for many women, that day may never come.

Small amounts *do* make a difference, as illustrated by the following table. Look what happens when $25, $50, and $100 is invested with an assumed return of 10% over time.

The Power of Time With Small Investments

	$25 per month	$50 per month	$100 per month
End of year 5	$2,015	$4,029	$8,059
End of year 10	5,259	10,519	21,037
End of year 20	10,485	20,790	41,940
End of year 25	32,455	64,909	129,818
End of year 30	54,283	108,566	217,132

Even if you wish you could put away $100 per month but you can only do $25 for now, it is still worth the effort. Think of it this way: Every amount you can accumulate will help provide you with a little more freedom and independence in the future.

Once you have begun the process and you can see and feel progress, you should increase the amount of savings as soon as possible, even if it's just by a couple of dollars. The woman who starts a disciplined savings and investment program early, even with small initial amounts, is far more likely to be successful at ensuring her future financial independence than the one who waits "until I can save enough to make a difference."

3. The Impact of Levels of Return on Your Investment

The example in the previous Time Value of Money section assumed an 8% per year average annual increase in the value of your investments. An 8% potential return could be a reasonable assumption for a balanced mix of stocks and bonds. If the investments were made primarily in stocks, a higher potential annual return, such as 10%, could be reasonable to assume. Let's look at what would happen if the same amount of money were getting a 10% average annual return.

Years	Total	Will Grow To
5	$10,000	$ 13,432
10	20,000	35,062
15	30,000	69,900
20	40,000	126,004
25	50,000	216,364
30	60,000	361,886
35	70,000	596,254
40	80,000	973,704

The difference between the 8% return and the 10% return after 20 years is $27,158. After 30 years the difference is $117,194!

This example illustrates the enormous impact that a change in investment strategy can have on the expected future value of savings and investments over a long period of time. When you are trying to accumulate a large amount of money for retirement, it is important to match the types of investments with the amount of time before the money will be needed. Usually the amount of money that must be accumulated for retirement is large enough that a conservative investment strategy, which is more appropriate for short-term needs, will not accomplish your goal. Most women have to be a bit more aggressive.

Investment Strategy Guidelines

The following general guidelines may help you choose an investment strategy that is appropriate for the amount of time needed when the goal is retirement income. Remember that the specific strategy that is right for you should be determined by you and your planner.

Strategy Chart

Guideline Description	Safety of Principal	Income/ Balanced	Growth	Total
Defensive	60%	30%	10%	100%
Conservative	40%	30%	30%	100%
Balanced	20%	40%	40%	100%
Growth	20%	30%	50%	100%
Aggressive	10%	20%	70%	100%

What does it all mean?

The vocabulary of investing can be a bit confusing because there are a couple of terms that have multiple meanings, depending on the context. "Balanced" and "growth" in the strategy chart are two such terms.

On this chart, the headings across the top describe *investments*, while the headings down the left column describe *investors*. Note that regardless of your characteristics as an investor, you will still have some percentage of your money in each of the investment categories. Reread the discussion about *diversification* and *asset allocation* in Chapter One if you are unclear about the reason for not putting all of your money in one investment.

Across the top

The terms "Safety of Principal," "Income/Balanced" and "Growth" all refer to the primary goal of various investments.

Safety of Principal means that the investment protects the dollar amount you put into it. When you cannot afford the possibility of losing the money you put into an investment, these are some of your choices:

- Money Market Accounts
- Savings Accounts
- Certificates of Deposit
- U.S. Savings Bonds
- Fixed Rate Annuities

The protection of principal for the investment choices noted are: FDIC insurance, faith and credit of the United States government, claims paying the ability of the insurer, penalties, insurance expenses, etc., depending on the investment.

Income/Balanced investments provide you with some income, and subject your principal to relatively low risk. In general, investments that can help achieve this include:

Government Securities (Treasury bills)
- Municipal Bonds
- Corporate Bonds
- Utility Stocks
- Preferred Stocks
- Balanced Funds (composed of bonds and high quality stock)
- Income-generating Real Estate
- Mortgage Securities (GinnyMaes)

Growth investments give your money—your principal—the opportunity to grow as much as possible. In order to achieve this, there is usually more risk involved. If you have at least 5-10 years before you will need the money you are saving, this is the category for you. The reason? Most growth investments are stock based, so they give you the highest probability of outpacing inflation and earning you more money than any other investment class. Investments in this category are:

- Individual Stocks
- Stock Mutual Funds (conservative to speculative)
- Mutual Funds that invest in specific sectors of the economy
- Mutual Funds that invest in international and global growth
- Real Estate held for appreciation

These lists are not precise, as some investments have characteristics of more than one category. For example, many stocks pay a dividend, therefore providing some income in addition to growth.

Down the Left Side

The left column of the strategy chart lists five adjectives to describe the various strategies you might adopt depending on your income needs, your risk tolerance and the time horizons for your financial objectives. In other words, they describe investors: *you.*

In general, the longer your time horizon for an investment, the more aggressive you can be. "Balanced," "Growth" and "Aggressive Growth" are appropriate when you have 5 to 10 years or more to invest. "Defensive" and "Conservative" are appropriate when you have a shorter time horizon, perhaps the purchase of a home or an expensive vacation you hope to take within the next few years.

When trying to locate yourself in this chart, remember that your risk tolerance is also a considerable factor. Your planner will help you establish where you are on the risk tolerance spectrum.

Because your personal strategy will be tied to your risk tolerance, and that probably will not change frequently, your strategy will not change often either. Furthermore, a change in the economy or in the stock market is usually not a reason to change your strategy. Long-term strategies take advantage of average returns over time and don't try to guess when the best and worst times will be.

The only valid reason for changing your strategy is if the time you will need your money changes. Keep in mind that when you have reached the date of retirement from employment, it does not necessarily mean that you should move to a more conservative strategy. A woman who is employed until age 65 still has a life expectancy of 19 years. And that's an average number; half of women age 65 will live more than 19 years. This is still a long time during which investments will need to provide income. Even at age 65, an investment strategy that focuses on growth is an important aspect of the financial plans of most women.

Finally, remember to consider all of your savings and investments, not just your personal ones. Any investment choices within a company retirement plan should also be included.

4. The Impact of Inflation on Investments

We are all aware of inflation when we purchase clothing or groceries. It's not difficult to think back a few years and recall how much you paid for an average grocery bill or a new suit. Or a new car. In fact, most things we buy continually get more expensive over time.

For some reason, it is more difficult to think about the "future" impact of inflation on retirement income in the same way. If inflation averages 5% per year, in 14½ years your average weekly grocery bill will double. The cost of a $30,000 car will be $60,000. Perhaps we don't think about inflation because while we are working, we expect to experience gradual increases in our income. And those increases, we hope, are allowing us to pay more for the things we buy.

But what happens at retirement? With no salary, our investments have to provide us with enough income to support us *and* they have to grow a little at the same time. Why? So that next year, when things cost a bit more, we will be able to cover the difference.

This is why even after retirement it is not wise to spend all of the income or return that your investments can produce. Some must be reinvested to help the investment gradually grow. For example, if you have investments that earn 9%, 3-4% of the total should be reinvested and only 5-6% should be spent. If you do not do this, you will be forced to gradually reduce your lifestyle because the same amount of earnings will buy you less and less each year.

The impact of inflation is another reason why a growth-oriented investment strategy is necessary for long-term needs such as retirement income. A strategy that is too conservative may provide a constant stream of income, but the purchasing power of that income will decrease each year. Soon, there will not be sufficient growth in the investments to try to turn the situation around and produce an increasing income stream.

5. Taxable vs. Tax-deferred Investing

The taxation of your investment earnings is an important factor in determining how far your investments will grow.

The following charts compare the results of investing in taxable investments and tax-deferred investments at various rates of return.

$1,000 Lump Sum Investment at 6%

	Taxable	Tax-deferred
Before-Tax %	6.00%	6.00%
After-Tax %*	4.00%	6.00%
End of year 5	$1,217	$1,338
End of year 10	1,480	1,791
End of year 15	1,801	2,397
End of year 20	2,191	3,207
End of year 25	2,666	4,292
End of year 30	3,243	5,743

*With an assumed federal income tax rate of 28% and an additional state income tax rate of 5% (which varies from state to state), the 6% return becomes an actual rate of 4% after taxes.

$1,000 Lump Sum Investment at 8%

	Taxable	Tax-deferred
Before-Tax %	8.00%	8.00%
After-Tax %*	5.33%	8.00%
End of year 5	$1,297	$1,469
End of year 10	1,681	2,159
End of year 15	2,180	3,172
End of year 20	2,827	4,661
End of year 25	3,666	6,848
End of year 30	4,753	10,063

*With an assumed federal income tax rate of 28% and an additional state income tax rate of 5% (which varies from state to state), the 8% return becomes an actual rate of 5.33% after taxes.

$1,000 Lump Sum Investment at 10%

	Taxable	Tax-deferred
Before-Tax %	10.00%	10.00%
After-Tax %*	6.67%	10.00%
End of year 5	$1,381	$1,611
End of year 10	1,907	2,594
End of year 15	2,633	4,177
End of year 20	3,636	6,727
End of year 25**	5,020	10,835
End of year 30	6,932	17,449

*With an assumed federal income tax rate of 28% and an additional state income tax rate of 5% (which varies from state to state), the 10% return becomes an actual rate of 6.67% after taxes.

**Note that at the 10% return rate, in 25 years the amount accumulated without tax is more than twice the amount accumulated with annual taxation on the earnings.

Tax-deferral means that you do not have to pay tax on your investment earnings each year. However, later, when you begin to withdraw income from the investments, the amount you withdraw *is taxable*.

Most of the savings plans established by an employer, such as the 401(k) plan, provide tax deferral on the investment earnings. For personal, non-employment related investing, a tax-deferred annuity, or an IRA, also provide tax deferral on investment earnings. This deferral of tax does have its price, though. In both the employment-related and personal tax-deferred annuities, if you take money out before you reach age 59½, you will have to pay the income tax due on the amount you have withdrawn and you will be assessed an additional 10% penalty on the amount withdrawn. The reason for the penalty is that these investment plans are designed to accumulate money for retirement; the penalty makes the pre-age 59½ withdrawal an expensive choice.

The Basics of Retirement Plans

The following are the main features of the most popular retirement plans that are provided by an employer and that you may be able to use individually. The purpose is to acquaint you with the characteristics of what may be available to you and to provide enough background so that you can feel comfortable asking further questions and participating in your plans.

The IRA

What is it?

An IRA is an Individual Retirement Account into which eligible individuals can contribute deductible or non-deductible payments. The payments will accumulate on a tax-deferred basis until payments are later withdrawn from the account.

An eligible individual is one who has earned income as an employee or self-employed person, or who receives alimony and has not yet reached age 70½. There are two types of IRAs: the Traditional IRA and the Roth IRA (for single people with under $100,000 income each year and married people with under $150,000 each year). The primary difference is that withdrawals from a Roth IRA are not subject to federal tax, while withdrawals from a Traditional IRA are taxed as current income.

How much can be invested?

The individual can contribute the lesser of $2,000 or 100% of compensation (earned income or alimony) in a year. If compensation is less than $2,000, only an amount equal to compensation can be contributed. As of this writing, there is pending legislation in Congress that would increase the amount of individual contributions to retirement accounts. The increase would take several years, and would make the new total $5,000.

How much is deductible?

The amount of deductible contribution allowed can be reduced or eliminated entirely if either the individual or her spouse is an "active participant." An "active participant" is a person who is eligible to participate in an employer-sponsored pension plan, a profit-sharing plan, a 401(k) plan, a stock bonus, a SEP plan, a tax-sheltered annuity, or any other government plan excluding Social Security, at any time during the year.

If either spouse was an active participant during the year, the amount of the Adjusted Gross Income on the joint tax return will determine how much of the IRA contribution is deductible. If a single person has an Adjusted Gross Income below $33,000, then a full $2,000 deductible IRA contribution is permitted. If the Adjusted Gross Income is above $43,000, no deductible contribution is permitted. Between $33,000 and $43,000, a pro-rata amount is allowed. For example, with Adjusted Gross Income of $35,000, the individual has exceeded the threshold by 20% ($2,000 above $25,000 and $8,000 less than $43,000) and could therefore contribute 80% of $2,000 ($1,600) on a deductible basis and 20% of $2,000 ($400) on a non-deductible basis.

For married taxpayers, the range of Adjusted Gross Income that determines how much of the IRA contribution that is deductible is $53,000 to $63,000. Below $53,000 of Adjusted Gross Income, the full $2,000 contribution is deductible even if either or both spouses were active participants during the year. Above $63,000, no deductible contribution is allowed if either spouse was an active participant during the year. In between, the pro rata portion of the $2,000 contribution is deductible.

It is important to remember that these limits are changed from time to time. In addition, if one spouse is eligible to make an IRA contribution and the other spouse has no income, a contribution can also be made into an IRA for the spouse with no income.

What are the tax advantages of an IRA?

IRAs, both deductible and non-deductible, accumulate without being taxed until withdrawals are made from the IRA (except in the case of the Roth IRA, where the withdrawals are tax free). As we have seen earlier in the chapter, the long-term advantage of tax-deferred accumulation is significant. Deductible IRAs have the added advantage of being deducted for current income tax calculations in the year of the contribution.

Once withdrawals from an IRA begin, only the amount withdrawn is taxed (again, not so for the Roth IRA). The portion remaining in the account continues to accumulate on a tax-deferred basis.

Are IRA withdrawals taxable?

When withdrawals are made from an IRA, they become taxable income. If withdrawals are made before age 59½, an additional penalty (10% of the amount withdrawn) must be paid. After age 59½, withdrawals in any amount are included in taxable income, but are not considered early withdrawals, so no penalty is assessed.

The only time early IRA withdrawals are not penalized is when they are for the purchase of a first home or because of a disability. The rule says that you may withdraw up to $10,000 (total) from your IRA for the purchase of a first home for yourself, your children, or your grand-children without incurring any penalties. If the IRA you are withdrawing from is a Roth IRA that is at least five years old, you can withdraw the money tax free *and* without an early withdrawal penalty. If you have a Traditional IRA you will be taxed on the withdrawal at your income tax rate at the time you took the withdrawal, but you will not owe a 10% early withdrawal penalty. You can also take early withdrawals if you are disabled.

It is also possible to take money out of an IRA before age 59½ with-out penalty if a special withdrawal calculation is done. This calculation is complicated and should not be attempted without professional help. However, in some situations, it can provide penalty free access to your IRA before age 59½. Make sure you know what kind of IRA you have and all of its rules, as some of those rules are very costly when you break them.

At age 70½, it is necessary to start making Required Minimum Distributions (RMDs) from your IRAs (excluding Roth IRAs), whether or not you need the money. The RMD is calculated using an age-based factor from a uniform table. (*Exception:* An account owner whose spouse is the sole beneficiary of his or her account is exempt from using the uniform table if the spouse is more than 10 years younger than the account owner. For this situation, RMDs may be based on the couple's longer joint life expectancy, allowing them to stretch out their distrib-utions over a longer period of time.) Once the required withdrawal amount is determined, the amount to be withdrawn can come from any of the accounts.

The SEP-IRA

What is it?

A SEP is a Simplified Employee Pension Plan. It is a type of IRA that can allow larger contributions than a regular IRA. The contribution is usually made by the employer and the employee owns the accounts. SEPs are often used by people who are self-employed and by people who have income from a second, part-time job.

How much can be invested?

A SEP will allow a tax-deductible contribution of up to 15% of the first $170,000 of income currently. (This contribution limit is gradually increasing.) Therefore, a woman making $40,000 can contribute up to $6,000 (15% of $40,000) to a SEP. If her business were structured as a Sole Proprietorship rather than a Corporation, she would be limited to about 13% of $40,000. In either case, the amount of tax-deductible contribution allowed can be is greater than with a regular IRA. A married woman can also establish a SEP on her own self-employed income regardless of whether or not her husband has a retirement plan through employment. This is not the case with the IRA, where eligibility depends on the level of Adjusted Gross Income on the joint tax return if the husband is an active participant.

Who is eligible to participate in addition to the employer?

If there are employees in the business, each full-time employee must be covered under the plan if the employee 1) is at least 21 years old, 2) has worked for the employer during the year for which the contribution is made *and* for at least three of the immediately preceding five years, and 3) has received at least $450 in compensation from the employer for the year. Even if an employee, because of death or termination of employment, is not an employee at the time the contribution is made, the employee must receive a plan contribution if the three criteria above are met. (The $450 amount of compensation factor is indexed and will gradually increase over time.)

The employer must make the same percentage contribution to all employees in a particular year. So if the employer decides to make a 10% contribution, all eligible employees must receive a contribution equal to 10% of their compensation. The employer can choose the level of contribution (between 0% and 15%) on a yearly basis.

The employee is 100% vested in the account balance immediately. If the employee leaves the employer, the full amount of the employee's account belongs to the employee.

What are the rules for withdrawals?

The rules for withdrawing funds from a SEP-IRA are similar to other IRAs: mandatory withdrawals starting at age 70½ and a 10% penalty for withdrawals prior to age 59½.

The Simple IRA Plan

What is it?

The Simple IRA Plan is a retirement plan designed for small business owners with 100 or fewer employees. It can also be used by a self-employed person.

How much can be invested?

With the Simple IRA, the employee can choose to defer from her paycheck a percentage of her salary or a flat dollar amount. The employee can defer up to 100 % of her income each year with a maximum contribution of $6,000 per year. (This limit will gradually be increased with inflation.)

The employer is required to make a contribution to the plan on behalf of the employee. This can either be a dollar-for-dollar match for participating employees of from 1% up to 3 % of the employee's compensation each year, up to $6,000 of employer contribution; *or* a flat 2% of compensation for all eligible employees. An eligible employee is one who has earned at least $5,000 in the current year whether or not she has participated in the tax-deferral plan available to her.

Who is eligible to participate?

To be eligible to participate in the Simple IRA, the employee must have 2 years of service during which she earned at least $5,000 per year, and is expected to earn at least $5,000 in the current year.

What are the rules for withdrawal?

Simple IRAs are like other IRAs in that you can withdraw funds after age 59½ and pay income tax on your withdrawal, but no penalty. Any withdrawals before age 59½ are subject to a 10% early withdrawal penalty. Simple IRAs have one additional twist on penalties. If the withdrawal is made within the first 2 years of participation, the withdrawal penalty is 25%.

What about vesting and required distributions?

Simple IRA plans require immediate 100% vesting of both the employer and employee contribution. This means that if you leave the employer, everything that both you and the employer contributed to your account is yours.

Like other IRAs, required distributions for Simple IRAs must begin at age 70½, and loans are not permitted.

The Pension Plan

What is it?

A pension plan is a retirement plan established and maintained by the employer. The plan will provide definitely determinable benefits to the employee in the future. The benefits will be paid to the employee for a specific number of years after retirement or for life.

How does it work?

The size of the employee's future benefit is determined by a formula that is fixed in advance by actuarial methods. The formula factors usually include the amount of the employee's compensation each year, the number of years of service, and the employee's age at retirement. According to the U.S. Labor Department, the median pension for women is half of the median pension for men. This is where you can clearly see the impact of moving in and out of the workforce and changing jobs.

There are two main types of corporate plans: ***defined benefit plans*** and ***defined contribution plans.***

The ***defined benefit plan*** is funded entirely by your employer. The amount of the contribution is based on the future total benefit and the employer makes the annual contribution each year that is needed to fund the future benefit that has been calculated in advance. And though inflation will erode your account over the years, a few large companies have a mechanism that automatically adjusts it for cost-of-living increases.

Depending on the details of your particular pension, you will probably be fully vested in anywhere from one to seven years. But that doesn't mean you should hop to a new job, wait till you are fully vested there, and move on again. Remember that time is what will grow your money. Even if you wait until you are fully vested to leave each of the jobs you have in, say, a decade, you still won't have as much money thirty years from now as if you had remained at one for that entire time.

The **defined contribution plan** is different in that the contribution to an employee's account each year is fixed or definitely determinable (rather than the future benefit). The amount of the contribution *cannot* be related to the company's profits. Usually it is a percentage of annual compensation, and that percentage is determined at the time the plan is established, and the same percentage is used each year.

At retirement, you receive whatever benefit can be provided by the funds that have accumulated in your account. In other words, you are not guaranteed an amount as you would be if you had a defined benefit plan. Furthermore, the funds inside a defined contribution plan account are all invested (either by you, the company, or both), which adds another element of uncertainty as to the amount you will end up with. It also adds market risk and other risks related to the specific investments into the mix.

What are the rules of eligibility?

Most pension plans require that the employee be at least 21 years old and have one year of service in order to be eligible to participate. A year of service is a 12-month period in which the employee worked at least 1,000 hours. In some cases, she may leave for a short period of time (e.g., to have a child) and get credit (but no new benefits) for the time she is gone. This helps her maintain the status of her pension.

What are the vesting schedules?

Pension plans must have vesting schedules that meet certain minimum requirements. This means that after participating in a plan for a certain number of years, the employee has a non-forfeitable right to the benefits that have accrued for her in the plan up to that point. If the employee leaves the employer after becoming vested, the employee will always have the right to the benefit accrued. Often the vesting schedule provides for partial vesting each year over a period of several years. So if an employee leaves before being 100% vested, there might still be a partial benefit available to her in the future.

It's worth stating the obvious: that the longer contributions are made on your behalf, the greater the future benefit will be. Even if you are 100% vested in a pension plan after five years of service, the future benefit from the plan is likely to be very small if you leave the employer and the plan after only five years. Remember that in a pension plan, the amount of future benefits depends on compensation level and years of service. Pension plans provide the greatest benefit to those who are long-term employees. If you leave or change employers shortly after becoming 100% vested, you will have a non-forfeitable right to a very small benefit.

When can payments start?

All pension plans must provide for a "Normal Retirement Date" that does not exceed age 65. The employee's right to a normal retirement benefit (based on the plan formula) must be non-forfeitable at the normal retirement date. Some plans provide for an earlier age as the normal retirement date if a certain number of years of service are attained by that earlier age.

Many plans also provide that an employee can take an early retirement benefit. This usually means that the amount of the benefit is reduced for every year of the difference between the normal retirement age stated in the plan and the early retirement age. For example, if a pension plan has a normal retirement age of 65 and a 3% per year reduction for each year of early retirement, an employee leaving at age 60 would experience a 15% reduction in her retirement benefit because of taking early retirement.

How are payments made from the pension plan?

The pension plan will specify the choices available for receiving benefits from the plan. Typically, a plan will make payments to the employee over the employee's lifetime or for a specified number of years. The size of the monthly retirement income payment is calculated according to a standard formula.

Some, but not all plans, will also allow the employee to choose that the benefits be paid out in a lump sum to her or to her IRA. If a lump sum distribution is taken from the plan, it is taxable to the employee if it is not rolled over to an IRA. If the lump sum is sent directly from the retirement plan to an IRA (without being payable to the employee), it is not taxable when it is moved to the IRA. Once in the IRA, the rules regarding taxation of withdrawals are the same as those discussed in the

IRA section of the chapter.

Pension plans require that benefits must be available to a surviving spouse at the participant's (employee's) death unless the surviving spouse waives his or her rights to these benefits in writing. The automatic payment of the retirement benefit is a *joint and survivor annuity.* This annuity provides that, at the death of the participant, a payment will continue to the spouse. That payment cannot be less than half of the amount received by the participant (employee). This form of annuity payment is often called a *joint and 50% survivor annuity* and is the minimum payment available to a spouse. This means that if the retirement plan paid $1,000 per month to the employee as a retirement income, the employee's spouse would receive $500 per month for the remainder of his or her life if the employee died first.

If the employee wants to make a payment choice that would pay more to the employee and less to the spouse as a survivor benefit, a written spousal waiver is needed. A *life annuity* would be a payment choice that requires a spousal waiver, as it pays the largest amount possible to the employee, but none to the spouse if the employee predeceases.

IRAs do not have provisions requiring spousal benefits. Therefore, if a lump sum distribution is taken from a pension plan (if permitted by the plan document) and rolled to an IRA, the spouse must consent. Once the money is in the IRA, the account owner (employee) can change the beneficiary as he or she wishes without regard to anyone else.

Profit-sharing Plans

What are they and how do they work?

Profit-sharing plans are retirement plans that allow the employer to share profits in the business with the employees. With profit-sharing plans, there is no predetermined formula for calculating a future benefit or for making contributions to the plan. Instead, the employer can decide each year how much can go into the plan from 0% up to 15% of the employee's compensation.

However, there must be a definite predetermined formula for *allocating* the funds that are contributed among eligible employees. Ordinarily, each employee receives the same percentage of compensation. If the employer decides to make a 5% of compensation contribution to the plan in a given year, each employee receives an amount equal to 5% of her own compensation in her own account.

At retirement, the size of the employee's account determines the size of the retirement benefit. The size of the account is determined by the amount paid in to the account over the employee's working years with the employer and the performance of the investments used in the plan.

What are the vesting, eligibility, retirement age and payment choices?

The provisions for vesting, eligibility, normal or early retirement age, and the types of payment choices available are generally the same for the profit sharing and pension plans.

401(k) Plans

What are they and how do they work?

401(k) plans are profit-sharing plans that allow the employee to contribute part of her income to the plan on a pre-tax basis. There may or may not be an employer contribution. If there is an employer contribution, it is in the form of a match of the employee's contribution, a typical profit-sharing type of contribution (such as 3% of each employee's compensation), or both.

The employer match is often something like $0.50 of each dollar the employee contributes, up to an 8% employee contribution. So an employee who contributes 8% of her salary would have an additional 4% contributed by the employer.

Often the employee can contribute up to 20% of her salary, although some employees are limited to a lower percentage, either by the plan itself or because they are in the group of "highly compensated" employees, and are therefore limited by the average contributions of the "other employees." There is also a dollar limit to the amount can be contributed by the employee each year. In 2001, the limit was $10,500. This amount gradually increases each year, and could be changed by new legislation.

What is the vesting schedule?

In a 401(k) plan, vesting is a little different from pension and profit-sharing plans because there are employee contributions. The employee is always 100% vested, from the beginning, in her own contributions. The normal types of vesting schedules discussed earlier apply to the employer contribution.

What are the eligibility, retirement age and retirement payment choices?

The provisions for eligibility, retirement age and retirement payment choices for 401(k) plans are very similar to these provisions in pension and profit-sharing plans.

What are the investment choices?

The investment of the funds in the 401(k) plan can be structured as "trustee directed" or "participant directed." When the investment decisions are trustee directed, the *employer* manages the investment or may have an investment manager do this. All employee funds are invested together, although each employee's account is allocated separately for reporting purposes.

In a participant-directed plan, each *employee* makes her own choices regarding the investment of her money in the plan. In many cases, there are a variety of investment choices made available to employees. The employee can often check on balances and make changes in investment choices through an 800 number.

In a participant-directed plan, each employee must take responsibility for determining her own investment strategy and implementing and monitoring her progress. In some participant-directed plans, the employee also makes the investment choices for the employer contribution to her account. In other words, the employee decides where the employer match will be invested.

What are the rules for loans and withdrawals?

Many 401(k) plans have a provision that allows a participant to withdraw funds from the plan under certain circumstances. In order to make a withdrawal, the employee must have an "immediate and heavy financial need" and be in a situation where other resources are not "reasonably available" to meet the need. The types of need that might qualify for this hardship withdrawal provision are:

1. Medical expenses
2. The purchase of a principal residence
3. Tuition and room and board for the next 12 months for an immediate family member
4. To prevent eviction from a principal residence or foreclosure of a mortgage on the principal residence

Hardship withdrawals are still taxable and may be subject to early withdrawal penalties if made before age 59½.

Some 401(k) plans will allow the employee to borrow money from the plan. The loans are limited in size and usually must be repaid at a stated interest rate over a 5-year period. The loan is repaid by payments that are deducted from the employee's paycheck and paid back into her 401(k) account. However, if the employee leaves employment with part of the loan unpaid, it will either have to be repaid at the time of leaving or the amount of the outstanding loan will be treated as a distribution on which she will have to pay tax and an early distribution penalty if she is younger than 59½.

Frequently Asked Questions About Retirement Plans

Every person who has a retirement plan should be able to answer all of these questions. Speak with your employer's benefits specialist to get all of the details of your plan.

1. At my death, what does my beneficiary get from my retirement plan?

The answer to this question has several parts and depends on the type of plan, who the beneficiary is and when death occurs.

If death occurs before retirement, the plan provisions determine what happens to an employee's account. Usually death means that the employee becomes 100% vested, if this were not the case prior to death. The account may be paid out to the beneficiary in the form of an annuity over the lifetime of the beneficiary, or in some cases, if the spouse is the beneficiary, the spouse can move the account into his or her own IRA. Sometimes the annuity payment to the spouse does not begin until the time when the employee would have been eligible for early retirement, had she lived. Often the spouse's benefit is the 50% benefit, which is the amount that a spouse would get under the joint and survivor annuity that would have been the automatic choice if the employee had lived and the spouse had not agreed to another choice.

There are a variety of possible payout arrangements to a spouse if the employee dies prior to retirement. It is important to check the plan description to know what would apply to you.

2. Can my retirement plan be owned jointly with my spouse?

No. The retirement plan must be owned by the person who generated the income needed to establish the account. At the death of the owner, if a rollover to an IRA is possible, the spouse could then become the new owner.

3. Can the employer use the money in the company retirement plan?

No. The funds in the plan are held in a trust and are for the benefit of plan participants and their beneficiaries.

4. What choices do I have when I leave an employer and I am ready to take income from my retirement plan?

The choices available for receiving money from a retirement plan are determined by the provisions of the plan. They can vary greatly from one plan to another, both between different companies and even between two different plans in the same company.

The two main types of distributions are the lump sum and the annuity payment. Some plans do not allow both types. Often, if the value of the plan account is below a certain amount, such as $3,500, it *must* be paid as a lump sum.

If a lump sum distribution is available, there are two choices to be made. If the distribution is paid out directly to the employee, it will be considered taxable income in the year of payment. If the employee is younger than 59½, the amount of the distribution is also subject to the 10% early distribution penalty. If the distribution is paid to the employee, the employer is required to withhold 20% of the distribution for income taxes before the remainder is distributed. It is possible to roll or move the distribution into an IRA within 60 days of receiving it and avoid taxation and penalty. However, the portion withheld by the employer for taxes is still considered a taxable distribution and may be subject to the penalty, depending on your age at the time.

In most cases, if a lump sum distribution is chosen, it is best to do a direct transfer into an IRA. This means that prior to the distribution, the employee decides where she wants the money to go and she establishes an IRA to hold the distribution. The employee then informs the employer or plan administrator how the distribution check should be written so that it will be deposited directly into the IRA and not come to the employee in the process. In this way, no taxes are required to be withheld by the employer, the distribution is not taxable, and the distribution is not subject to an early distribution penalty.

In some cases, it is possible to move the distribution from the plan of a prior employer into the plan of a new employer. For this to be possible, the plan of the new employer must include a provision allowing this type of transfer.

If a lump sum distribution is not available or not desired, an annuity payment would be chosen. Usually, an annuity payment would not start until the employee would be old enough to be eligible for retirement from the employer. Again, this age varies from plan to plan.

When an annuity payment amount is listed on a company benefit statement, it is often the "life annuity" amount. This is the largest annuity payment that could be paid to the employee and will be paid for that employee's lifetime, regardless of how long she lives. If the employee lives to normal life expectancy or beyond, the full value of her accrued account would be paid out. However, if she lives only a short time beyond retirement, only a small portion of the accrued account would be paid out, and the remainder would be forfeited.

In order to avoid the problems of a potentially short payout period (if the employee dies prematurely), several other payout choices are available. These would make payments to a spouse for his lifetime if the retired employee predeceases or would make payments to someone, either a spouse or other beneficiary, for a stated number of years.

Because of the ongoing payments beyond the life of the retired employee, any of the above methods will mean that the payment to the retired employee will be less than the life annuity amount.

Joint and Survivor Payments

The two most common types of joint payments are the "joint and 50% survivor" payment and the "joint and 100% survivor" payment. The joint and 50% survivor payment will pay a reduced amount to the retiree, and if the retiree predeceases, 50% of the retiree's amount is paid to the surviving spouse. The amount of the retiree's reduction, compared to the life annuity amount, is often about 10%, although it can vary depending on the plan and the difference in the ages of the spouses.

The joint and 100% survivor payment requires a greater reduction in payment to the retiree (usually about 20% less than the life annuity amount, although this can again vary from plan to plan and also depends greatly on the age difference of the spouses), but will pay the same amount to the surviving spouse that the retiree received, if the retiree predeceases.

Usually, with joint and survivor payments, if the spouse predeceases, the reduced amount payable to the retiree cannot be increased back up to the life annuity level. Therefore, the health of the spouse at the time a payment choice is made is an important factor.

When the payment choice is made it is almost always irrevocable. If the retiree is married at the time that a payment is to begin, the automatic choice must be the joint and 50% survivor option unless the spouse is willing to agree to a different choice in writing, if the choice would pay less to the survivor. The joint and 100% survivor benefit would pay more to the surviving spouse than the joint and 50% survivor payment. But the life annuity payment would pay nothing to a surviving spouse and cannot be chosen without the spouse's written consent.

There are often several payment choices that will pay for the life of the retiree, and at least for a certain number of years, such as 10, 15, or 20 years. One of these choices is often made if there is not a spouse, but there is a desire to have the payments made to someone if the retiree lives only a short time after retirement. For example, a widowed retiree might make a "life and 10-year certain" choice. This would mean that the payments would continue to her for life, but if she should die five years after retirement, the payments would continue to her beneficiary for five more years, so that a minimum of 10 years of payments would be made to someone.

Each choice that provides a potential benefit to someone other than the retiree means a reduction in the retired employee's amount from the maximum life annuity amount.

Over the course of their working lives, many women will have benefits from several employer-sponsored retirement plans. Each plan could have different provisions different payout choices could be made from each plan. Although this mixture can be complicated, it is important to be aware of the possible choices for each plan that will provide retirement benefits. It is also critical to coordinate the choices for the payment of benefits from various plans.

5. What are required minimum withdrawals from retirement plans?

As you know, money in retirement plans is not subject to income tax, either when the money is contributed to the plan, or as it grows in the plan. However, the rules regulating taxation of retirement plans dictate that eventually the money in these plans must be taxed. If the money is taken out as an annuity payment, each payment is taxed as income when it is received. If the money is in an IRA, at age 70½ it is necessary to calculate *Required Minimum Distributions* each year. This required minimum is the smallest amount that must be withdrawn from the IRAs each year and counted as taxable income for the year. It is always possible to take out more than the minimum if desired.

The penalty for not taking a large enough withdrawal from the retirement accounts is large. Normal income tax plus a 50% penalty must be paid on any amount that should have been withdrawn but was not.

6. What happens when I change jobs?

Changing jobs usually has a negative impact on the benefits you will receive from your employer-sponsored retirement plans, unless you are moving from an employer with no plan or a poor plan, to an employer with a better plan.

In most cases, you must be employed for a year before you can participate in the retirement plan provided by the employer. Therefore, changing jobs often can mean many one-year periods with no retirement plan contribution being made for you.

If your retirement plan has a vesting schedule, as most do, leaving before you are 100% vested (which can take as long as seven years and sometimes longer) means that you will not receive all of the funds in your account. The part in which you are not vested remains in the plan and is allocated to those employees who remain with the employer. Again, changing jobs frequently means that you never get the full benefit of contributions made for you by the employer.

If the employer has a defined benefit pension plan, the formula determining the benefit is often designed to benefit long-term employees. The employees who do not stay long usually get small benefits in the future from a defined benefit pension plan.

7. What is a rollover?

A rollover is the transfer of a distribution from a retirement plan, a tax-sheltered annuity, or an individual retirement plan (IRA) into another individual retirement plan account. This transfer is nontaxable if certain rollover rules are followed. When a transfer from a retirement plan of the employer is made to a personal IRA, it is important that the transfer be a *direct transfer* in order to avoid taxation and tax withholding.

If the transfer is made from one IRA to another, the transfer is non-taxable and does not require withholding as long as the funds are deposited into a new IRA within 60 days of being withdrawn from the prior IRA. As long as the amount deposited in the new account is the same amount as was withdrawn from the old one, there is no taxable transfer.

If the funds had some earnings during the transition period, the earnings are not included in the new account, but are taxable earnings in the year of the transfer. In making a transfer from one IRA to another, it is possible to instruct the trustee of the old account to send money directly to the new trustee without being sent to the IRA owner in the process. This type of transfer is called a Trustee-to-Trustee transfer.

8. Can I borrow money from my retirement plan if I need it?

Some employer-sponsored plans (usually 401(k) plans) have a provision that allows an employee to borrow from the account if certain requirements are met. In general, if loans are allowed they must be paid back within five years, and there is a dollar limit to the amount that can be borrowed. Normally, the employee cannot borrow more than 1/2 of her non-forfeitable benefit (vested amount) in the plan and this cannot exceed $50,000. If these rules are violated, a taxable distribution has occurred.

The plan document itself describes whether loans are permitted, and if they are, it describes the provisions. If you are at all unsure about these provisions, ask for a copy of the "Summary Plan Description." As a participant, you are entitled to a copy of this information.

It is not possible to borrow from a Traditional IRA without a financial penalty. Any withdrawals will be considered taxable distributions. Eligible withdrawals from the Roth IRA are not subject to federal tax, however (although some states tax them).

9. What are my rights if my spouse has a retirement plan?

If your spouse has an employer-sponsored retirement plan, you must be the beneficiary of that plan unless you have consented, in writing, to waive your rights to the survivor benefits in the plan. (See Question 4.)

10. What kinds of retirement plans can I have if I am self-employed?

Many self-employed people use a SEP, or Simple IRAs, described earlier in this chapter. These plans are easy to establish and administer and are especially attractive for the self-employed person who either has no employees or has a limited number of long-term employees.

It is also possible for the self-employed person to use a profit-sharing plan, a money purchase pension plan, or a combination of the two. These plans can provide a larger contribution than the SEP or Simple Plan, but are more expensive to administer.

It is important for the person who is self-employed to plan on establishing a retirement plan as one of the normal expenses of running the business.

Questions to Ask About Your Retirement Plan

Before you take a new job, make sure you get satisfactory answers to all of these questions.

- What types of retirement plans does the company offer?
- When will I be eligible to participate?
- Can I contribute to the plan? If so, how much?
- Are all of my contributions paid in before-tax dollars?
- What are my investment choices?
- How often can I change the amount of my contribution or my investment choices?
- Is there a vesting schedule for the employer contributions? If so, what is it?
- Is it possible to borrow money from my retirement plan account? If so, how much can be borrowed? What are the terms?
- What is the "Normal Retirement Age" for the retirement plan?
- Is there a provision for early retirement? What age is possible for early retirement? How is the retirement benefit reduced for early retirement?
- What payment choices are available at retirement? Is a lump sum distribution an option?
- If I die before retirement, what benefit is payable to my beneficiary? When?
- Who manages the money in the retirement plan? What is the

investment policy of the fund? What investments are in the retirement fund?

- Would you please provide me with a copy of the Summary Plan Description of the retirement plan?

Conclusion

Your retirement is the single aspect of your financial life that will require the most preparation time. In fact, in order to make the most of it, you should have begun saving for retirement with your first paycheck.

I realize that very few people actually do that, but if you are among the millions who didn't, that doesn't mean you cannot have a comfortable retirement. What it does mean is that planning is very important. This chapter has introduced you to the basic elements of retirement planning that will allow you to thoroughly understand what your financial planner will discuss with you.

The most important tips to remember are:

- **Start saving as early as possible** (i.e., NOW!) Even if you are unable to save as much as you would like to at first, it is more important to get accustomed to setting some money aside, regardless of how much. In the beginning, the discipline of saving is more important than the actual amount saved. Determine an amount you feel comfortable starting with, talk to your planner about which investment is best for you, and make the investment amount the very first bill you pay each month.

   Better yet, arrange for the chosen amount to go automatically from your account to the investment each month. Most people are more successful with an automatic system because there are no choices involved; they are not tempted to opt to put the money elsewhere. In my experience, very few people, even those with high incomes, have anything "left over" at the end of the month except good intentions.

- **Allocate a certain percentage of your current income toward savings and investments for the future.** For most people, it takes about 15% of their income over a period of 20 to 30 years in order to accumulate enough for retirement. It is important to plan on a percentage rather than just a dollar amount. This way, as your income increases, the actual dollars allocated to long-term savings and investments increase, as well.

- **Choose an investment strategy that emphasizes growth for long-term accumulation.** The more risk you can take, the greater the potential for your money to grow. Your planner will help you determine your risk tolerance. If your risk tolerance is particularly low, the percentage of your money that will be allocated to investments involving more risk (i.e., the stock market) will be low.

- **Choose an investment strategy that fits your time horizon and is likely to give you the return you need to achieve your goals.**

- **Use tax-deferred investments as much as possible when accumulating for retirement.** Ask your planner about which personal investments would allow you to contribute before-tax dollars.

- **Make sure you know exactly what is available from your employer and the employer of your spouse or partner.** Very few people are knowledgeable about this critical aspect of their financial lives and futures. Many times this is because when they try to get the information from the employer, they get an incomplete answer. If this happens to you, be persistent. You have the right to know every detail about what affects your financial life, and you should not stop asking until the answers you get are satisfactory to you and your planner. Use the list of questions in the previous section as a guide.

- **Take full advantage of all employer-sponsored plans.** Contribute the maximum amount allowed, not just the amount needed to receive an employer match.

- **If you are looking for a job, seek an employer who has a retirement plan that allows you to contribute on a before-tax basis and who adds to the plan himself.**

- **Congratulate yourself for taking responsibility for your financial future.**

All of the figures quoted in the charts in this chapter are for illustrative purposes only and are not necessarily indicative of past of future results of any specific investment. They do not include consideration of the time value of money, inflation, fluctuation in principal, or in many instances, taxes.

All material discussed in this chapter is meant for general illustration and/or information purposes only and it is not to be construed as investment advice. Although the information has been gathered from sources believed to be reliable, it cannot be guaranteed. Please note that individual situations can vary; therefore, the information should be relied upon when coordinated with individual advice.

Chapter Five

Divorce

By Cicily Maton, CFP™

> The average woman's standard of living drops 45% in the
> year following a divorce, while a man's rises 15%.
> —The National Center for Women and Retirement
> Research at Long Island University.

If divorce is a possibility for you, reprimanding yourself for all of the bad
choices you have made (and most of them probably didn't seem too bad
at the time) is not productive. Instead, you must immediately take steps
to protect your financial future and your emotional state. Your first step
is to learn about what the divorce process looks like and how you can
best prepare yourself for it.

This chapter will give you step-by-step instructions to help you
organize your life in preparation for your meetings with your financial
planner and attorney regarding your divorce negotiations. Your settlement will consist of property, perhaps maintenance, and child support
if you have minor children. I will explain what these three items mean
to you financially so you are in the best position to get down to business
when you begin your negotiations.

My intention is to create a picture of the landscape you are enter-
ing. Unfortunately, it is not very pretty, it is very technical and it often
doesn't seem fair. And it's not just about money. Your financial passage
through divorce is inextricably linked to your emotional passage. In
order for your financial and emotional life to emerge healthy and
whole, you need to take care of them from the beginning. Taking care
involves learning as much as you can about the process you are going
through so you will not be taken by surprise (as much) and you will have
a clear view to the light at the end of the tunnel.

Don't Assume You are Going to Court

About 95% of divorces are settled out of court. That's a positive statistic, as it means that most couples can agree on an arrangement without a judge having to intervene. What's even more promising is that mediation, sometimes called *alternative dispute resolution*, is increasingly common.

Mediation should be the first option of couples who have some degree of trust and who share common goals, such as the preservation of harmony in order to raise the children in a positive environment. It is a voluntary process wherein both spouses cooperate and collaborate on creating their legal separation. The mediator's job is to facilitate the discussion to shape a solution to the issues in dispute. From financial property settlement to maintenance and child support to parenting agreements, many mediators are trained to handle all of the aspects of your divorce. And many financial planners and divorce lawyers are also trained divorce mediators.

However, whether or not you are choosing mediation, you still need a good lawyer on your team of advisors, for two reasons. First, because it is the job of the mediator is to remain neutral, and you need someone who is an adversary on your behalf. Second, because most mediators are *not* lawyers, they ordinarily do not have knowledge of case law. If there is a dispute over a statute, an interpretation, or another detail of law or process, a mediator is not likely to be able to help, but a lawyer is trained to be aware of all pertinent matters and knows how to handle them.

If you do not know whether mediation will be a viable option for you, read through the following list of warning signs. If you answer "yes" to any of these questions, you could be in for a battle.

- Is either of you likely to want to use the legal system to "get even?" (If so, get ready for an expensive and drawn out fight.)
- Is either of you a lawyer or an entrepreneur?
- Do either of you own a cash business or travel abroad often?
- Do either of you have a controlling personality?

If you answered yes to any of the above, I suggest you prepare yourself for a divorce action. And the best way to do that is to assemble an expert team of professionals and prepare for trial. I'll tell you what experts you need and show you how to find them, and I'll explain how you can prepare yourself for your road ahead. By being prepared, you stand an excellent chance of settling long before you go to trial.

Divorce is a Legal Process

Divorce is a legal process where one party files for divorce, and the other party answers the suit, usually filing a counter suit. But none of that tells you what is really going on. At some point during all of the legalities that accompany being party to a lawsuit, reality sets in, and you usually begin to feel like you have lost control of your life.

By this time you and your ex-to be have probably hired lawyers who have sworn to protect *your* interests. Remember that lawyers are, by training, adversarial. The very fact that lawyers aggressively protect your rights can fan the flames of anger, hurt and misunderstanding. If you do not have a therapist to help you through your emotional divorce, you should seriously consider getting one.

Emotional Divorce

While the technical divorce may be legal, there is also an emotional divorce going on, and it can be intensely destructive. Almost everyone who goes through a divorce is temporarily insane. Almost everyone, on both sides, is under a great deal of stress and believes that the other side is "out to get" them. Almost everyone is paranoid that the mail is being opened, the phone is being tapped, they are being followed and their garbage is being rifled. And in reality, almost everyone is wrong.

Nevertheless, each side experiences its own set of ups and downs, and always maintains that the other side has the upper hand. Therapists are well aware of the range of emotions experienced by those in the throes of divorce. Therapists know that only the death of a child or a spouse compares to the stress and emotional turmoil of divorce.

I strongly advise that you do yourself a favor and immediately seek out a therapist who specializes in divorce and separation. The stress and the range of emotions that you will experience should be shared with a professional who can help you cope, speed your recovery time, and launch you into your new life once the divorce is behind you.

Financial Divorce

Despite hurt feelings and anger that runs deep, in the final analysis, divorce is really about the money. It may be a legal process fought in an environment of emotional trauma, but the battlefield is money. Don't believe anyone who tells you otherwise.

Once you embrace that reality, your strategy should be to move as quickly as you can to a meaningful dialogue to solve the economic issues. The process will be less costly, and you both can go on with your new lives.

The Final Settlement

The final settlement will weave together three possible financial pieces of the puzzle: property division, maintenance (also known as *alimony*) and child support. Property is always part of the settlement, but maintenance is not. Maintenance is more like a swing item that can make a situation more equitable. If, for instance, the factors show that one of the spouses has a disproportionate share of property, maintenance may be awarded to the disadvantaged spouse as a trade-off.

While the factors governing the property division and the awarding of maintenance and child support are spelled out separately, they are all combined and evaluated as the final settlement package. And in order to reach that, most couples need to enlist the aid of an objective third party: either a mediator or a judge (and again, you should also have your own attorney).

When Mediation Isn't Possible

Although mediation is a very nice idea, it is impossible for some couples, and those couples usually know who they are. If the relatively congenial, cooperative atmosphere of mediation isn't an option for you, divorce is inevitable, and it could get nasty. If you do not already have a lawyer who is qualified to represent you in your divorce, and with whom you are comfortable, you are going to have to do some research. Here's how . . .

- Compile a list of recommendations from friends, colleagues, the yellow pages, the bar association and even your hairdresser.
- Organize your financial information and summarize the personal information about your family that will help the lawyer understand your case (a detailed explanation of what you will need is upcoming).
- Write a list of questions for each of the lawyers you will interview. Bring the list with you to each meeting, record the interviewee's answers, and compare your results after you have conducted all of the interviews. Some questions at the top of

your list should be:

» How much is your retainer? Is it refundable if you do not use it at all?

» What is your hourly fee?

» When am I expected to pay my bill when the retainer runs out?

» Will my husband have to pay my attorney fees?

» How often will I receive a bill?

» What is your policy on returning phone calls?

» Will associates in your office work on my case? If so, what will they charge me? Do you work with financial planners? Mediators?

» How much of your practice is divorce?

» What percent of your cases are settled out-of-court? How many go to trial?

Unfortunately, you cannot expect precise answers to questions such as, "How long will it take, what will I get, and how much will it cost?" The legal process is slow and the courts are overloaded, so expect delays. Most lawyers will give you a range of possibilities as to the final financial outcome.

Once you have interviewed your list of lawyers, compare their answers and choose the person you believe will best serve your interests. The more information you have before meeting with a lawyer, the better prepared you will be to ask the right questions and to make a wise choice. Your financial planner will be able to help you sort through the financial details so you will be equipped to explain your situation to your attorney.

Finding a Financial Planner

If you have not been the major financial decision maker in your marriage, you can easily feel overwhelmed when you are faced with making such decisions for the first time. And when you add divorce into the mix, your confusion can multiply. Even the most financially sophisticated women find their decision-making skills are impaired during the emotional turmoil of divorce. If you aren't financially savvy already, going through a divorce without a financial planner who is an expert in divorce can be disastrous. At best, you will be at a disadvantage.

I recommend finding a financial planner as early as possible because as you and your team make offers and receive proposals during the negotiation stage of your divorce, you are going to have to evaluate those proposals. A financial planner can reduce each different option to a specific dollar amount. Each option can then be viewed in terms of the future stream of payments of maintenance and/or child support, so you can easily evaluate it. This calculation is not an easy one and is best done by an expert. That expert can also advise you about other merits of each proposal you receive during your negotiations.

The Pros and Cons of Remaining in the Workforce

Whether or not to remain in the workforce and/or pursue a full-time career is a quandary many divorcing women are faced with. Many professional and career women enter the process with more confidence than homemakers. But a career can actually be a double-edged sword when you are in the midst of a divorce. Many career women find that they are expected to pay maintenance (or alimony) to a lower-wage earning or unemployed spouse. They are also challenged for custody of their children because they don't have enough time and are not receiving credit for doing *double duty.*

Many career women are advised to quit to avoid this bind, but that often creates a different problem. If a major wage earner has blatantly curbed their income, the court could compute their income as if they had continued to work.

And women who are *not* employed are also in a bind because they are often advised not to take a job as that might lower their maintenance award. But divorce sometimes lasts three or four years! Meanwhile, the woman has delayed her career, has had no income, and is probably stewing in her anger because she has much more time to do so. My advice? Take courses, do some career counseling, get a personal coach and prepare yourself for your new life. Get out of the house and do something positive for your future and get ready to support yourself. And if a great job comes you way, think about the big picture and what the job will do for you in the long run.

My recommendation is always to make informed choices. Whatever you choose to do with your career or your personal life, that choice should be made only after you have examined the consequences of your options. Too often, I see women making decisions based on how they feel the moment they are faced with a choice. My motto is: Whenever possible, do not make a choice until you are doing so based on the facts instead of how you are feeling.

Preparation for Your Negotiations

Gather Financial Documents

Your first task *before* you meet with your planner and your attorney should be to gather all of your financial documents. You, your attorney, and your financial planner will organize all of your documents into "facts" and "proof" to substantiate your case. Remember, divorce is a legal process and there are methods and procedures that must be followed by your team to prepare the best case for you. You will not be awarded anything unless you prove that you deserve it. Your financial documents consist of:

- At least five years of past tax returns
- At least two years of canceled checks and bank statements
- Credit card statements
- Copies of brokerage account statements
- IRA paperwork
- Documents from benefits such as 401(k), employee savings, defined benefits and stock options
- Most recent pay stubs
- Life insurance policies
- Mortgage papers
- Closing papers from real estate purchases
- Limited partnership papers
- Employment contracts
- Anything that relates to what you and your spouse own, owe, earn, or spend

Do not worry at this data gathering stage whose name is on the title, who ran up the debts, or who earned the money. Your attorney and your financial planner will help you sort all that out later.

Organize all the documents in file folders and keep them in a safe place. Do not hand over original documents to anyone; it is too easy for them to get misplaced. Instead, make copies for your advisors.

Secure Temporary Support

Securing temporary support is the single most important strategic step in the divorce process, and you should do it as early as possible. One of the primary reasons that there are so many stories about the gross inequities in divorce settlements is the imbalance of power between the spouses. The imbalance of power (especially economic power) often occurs when one spouse is the primary caregiver and not in the workforce full time. The traditional caregiver—the woman—is almost always the physical custodian of the children. As a result, she is often totally dependent on her husband—the major wage earner—to pay the bills.

Even if you are not worried about being thrown out of the house because you can't pay the mortgage, you will not be in an equal position to negotiate if you don't have enough money and your husband is free to continue his lifestyle without restraint.

If you are the major wage earner, your concern is that you not be overburdened with family support while your husband assumes no responsibility. If you are the dependent spouse, you need to protect yourself and insure that you are adequately supported until the conclusion of the divorce. The best way to do that is to insist that your attorney get a temporary support order. The procedure for securing this support begins with the completion of an affidavit of income and expenses. You may be asked to supply as much other financial information as you have (listed above). Be prepared to go to court and appear before a judge to prove your case. Your objective will be to provide evidence for the standard of living you and your family had prior to the breakdown of the marriage. You will also submit your current needs (i.e., your budget) and the ability of your husband to pay.

Your husband's attorney, on the other hand, will be trying to prove that:

a) Your standard of living is inflated, and you spend too much on _____ (you fill in the blank—or blanks) and;
b) Your husband cannot afford to pay enough to support you and the children at the level you claim you need.

How to Handle Your Husband's Objections

I recommend taking all of the guesswork out of your request for temporary support by producing an historical analysis of your cash flow. If you are comfortable with computers, use a money management program such as Quicken® to input each check and each credit card expenditure. Code them by categories such as: housing, food, auto, children, etc... for a period of at least one year prior to the breakdown of the marriage. If you do not want to use a computer, you can do the same record keeping with a ledger pad. Either way, this is a time-consuming and detailed report to produce, and you will probably need the assistance of your planner to complete it.

This historic spending pattern can then be summarized in one or two pages for the judge to review. At a glance, it should be evident what you and your family spend to maintain your standard of living. This simple report will eliminate all fighting about the standard of living and make it easier for the trial court to make a decision in your favor.

Using the historic spending levels as a base, complete an item-by-item evaluation of your current needs. There may be some categories that have increased or decreased. Make notes as to why you have deviated from the historic number. Keep this worksheet and include it in the full report compiled for the hearing on temporary support.

Prove Your Case

The full report that is compiled in anticipation of a hearing will be voluminous. The report should include seven to ten sections, depending on your circumstances:

1) An affidavit of needs
2) The worksheet (or computer printouts) that estimated the current needs that were recorded on the affidavit
3) A summary of annual expenditures for one, two, or three years
4) A detailed list of expenditures by individual categories
5) A detailed list of transactions for the period covered
6) Copies of bank statements of the accounts included in the reports
7) Copies of the credit card statements included in the reports

You will need copies for yourself, your financial planner, your spouse, your spouse's attorney and the judge. If you and your team have spent the time and the money to compile a report that is this detailed and verifiable as "proof," you may not ever have a court hearing. By preparing for the worst, you most often can avoid it. If the other side knows that the trial judge is most likely to award a temporary award that is substantiated by a cash flow analysis, they will make a deal.

Warning! Do not cut or reduce your monthly budget because you think that temporary support is only temporary. Even though many lawyers will tell you that temporary awards are made "without prejudice," the temporary award is seldom increased in the final agreement. On the other hand, do not inflate your needs. If you do, your husband's attorney is likely to use it against you and discredit you to convince the judge that your "needs" are unrealistic and not justified.

The Rules: Divorce Law

As I said at the beginning of the chapter, most couples agree on a property settlement without having to go to trial. Only about five percent of divorce actions result in a trial. But whether they are negotiated, mediated, or mutually agreed upon, property settlements must have a recognized authoritative standard to establish guidelines for the negotiations. Statutes within each state and case law provide that standard.

Your attorney, your husband's attorney and your trial judge all make their decisions based on something you probably don't have: knowledge about the laws that govern divorce proceedings. These laws have changed as our society has evolved, and it would behoove you to learn about the law so you will be able to work most effectively with your divorce attorney and your financial planner.

There is No Fault

The practice of proving blame (i.e., *fault*) before one could get a divorce came under attack in the 1970s. California was the first state to pass no-fault divorce. Many divorce lawyers thought that the process of proving which spouse was the one causing the breakdown of the marriage was time-consuming, costly, counterproductive and not in the best interest of the family unit. The assumption was that if couples could concentrate on the financial division of the marital assets, the whole divorce would not take as long and would not be as costly, and that hopefully, it would not leave one of the spouses with the social stigma of being the cause of the divorce.

Fault and no-fault as grounds for divorce is currently being discussed in academic circles by divorce lawyers and by many state legislatures around the country as the root cause of the decline in the standard of living experienced by many women following divorce. Some state legislatures are now considering repeal or modification of the no-fault provision.

Regardless of the current debate on the status of no fault as grounds for obtaining a divorce, as it now stands, in all but a few states, fault has no bearing on the division of property.

Federal Law

Federal law will apply in divorce cases in a number of areas. Foremost is the treatment of income taxes relating to divorce. In addition, over the years following the adoption of the equitable distribution system, a number of inequities began to appear that were corrected by federal law.

Taxes

Federal tax law applies in the treatment of property transferred between spouses incident to a divorce. The Federal IRS Tax Code determines the application of income taxes on maintenance and child support. In the minefield of financial issues facing you, don't overlook opportunities to save tax dollars by using the tax code to your advantage.

In general, maintenance is a deduction to the payee and taxable to the recipient. Child support is a direct transfer and is not a deduction to the payer nor is it taxable income for the parent receiving it. The IRS has a number of booklets that deal with the special rules for divorced and separated individuals, and your local IRS office can provide copies. IRS Publication 504, for Divorced or Separated Individuals, is especially helpful.

State Law

State law governs the process of the legal divorce. The statutes of each state spell out the factors that are to be considered and weighed in determining an equitable division of assets. These factors vary from state to state, and many of them are discussed below. In addition, the states differ on whether the court's consideration of the factors is mandatory or discretionary. The only thing all states require of the court is to *consider* the factors; the weight given each factor is at the discretion of the trial court. Trial court decisions are overturned only for clear abuse of discretion.

The classification of property is the most important set of distinctions to understand. Everything you and your husband own will be classified as marital property, non-marital property, or separate property. What property goes to whom is spelled out in your state's statutes, and there may be exceptions and interpretations that are unique to your state. Keep in mind that the law is subject to constant change in response to new legislation and case law. This reality makes it even more important to research exactly what you are up against if you are faced with the prospect of divorce. As it stands in 2001:

- **Marital property** is generally all property acquired *during* the marriage.
- **Non-marital property** or **separate property** is property acquired by gift, inheritance, or owned *before* the marriage.
- **Community property** is all property acquired *during* the marriage and each spouse is an equal owner of the property.

How each of these distinctions affects you depends on where you live. As of 2001, there are nine community property states (Arizona, California, Idaho, Louisiana, Nevada, New Mexico, Texas, Washington, and Wisconsin). If you live in one of these states, all of your marital assets will be divided evenly between you and your husband. That is assumed to be the most equitable arrangement, and if you disagree it is up to you to prove why you are entitled to more of the pie.

Forty other states use the principle of equitable distribution, which I will discuss in a moment. Finally, in Mississippi, and only in Mississippi, you will keep the property that has a title with your name on it, and your husband will keep the property that is titled with his name. The best way to find out exactly how your state deals with family law is to get a copy of your state's statutes as soon as possible. You can do this on the Internet at www.divorcecentral.com and many other web sites that list each states current laws regarding divorce.

What's all this about "equitable distribution?"

Just what does equitable distribution mean? Unfortunately, the law does not provide a definition. Despite the fact that the courts have been making decisions based on equitable distribution for nearly 20 years, there is no standard formula. Case law provides precedents, but with the infinite variety of factors that can occur, the final definition is at the discretion of the trial court. Equitable distribution essentially means that the trial court is supposed to apply a "fair and reasonable" standard to the relevant criteria (*factors*) that are found in state statutes (and are described below).

While there is no agreement on a definition for "equitable," there is uniform agreement, in both common law and community property states, on the application of the partnership theory to the division of marital property.

Partnership Theory

Marriage is viewed very much like a partnership in a business venture. At divorce, the "partners" divide the "profits" of the business venture, that is, the marital property. The conflict is in determining what defines property and what each of the partners will get.

Under the partnership theory, it is a given that each partner has an interest in the property of the partnership. The interest in the property of the partnership is based on each partner's contribution. Contribution, in the context of marriage and divorce, encompasses both direct economic contributions and non-economic contributions of a non-working spouse.

Contributions by the spouses to specific marital assets are included in all state statutes. The wording varies from state to state, but Illinois' statute is typical and was based on the Uniform Marital Property Act.

> Ill. Rev. Stat. Ch. 40, D 503(d)(1) " . . . the contribution of each spouse to the acquisition, preservation, or increase or decrease in value of the marital and non-marital property, including the contribution of a spouse as a homemaker or to the family unit . . ."

The language is so broad to allow for the wide variety of contributions that may be applicable. Most statutes expressly include homemaker contributions. The weight given those contributions depends on other factors.

Some of the Factors that Will be Considered

It is the responsibility of each side to present the relevant factors to the court. Factors not in evidence most likely will be given little or no weight in property division. Consideration of all relevant factors in a case is equally important in mutual agreements, mediation, or negotiated settlements. It is essential to establish the reasonable needs of *both* spouses. Only then does the trial court have the necessary data to balance the relevant resources between the parties.

Some of the factors that will be considered are:

- **Direct contributions by the parties to marital assets**
  Direct financial contributions are given considerable weight, although general non-economic contributions to the marital partnership are also recognized by most of the states. The most important non-economic contribution is homemaker services,

and they are relevant in the discussion of equitable distribution.

The problem is that the weight of this non-economic factor is not easily quantified. And in order to arrive at an equitable division of property, all of the factors must be quantified. Some states avoid the arduous task of measuring the economic value on the contributions of a homemaker. Instead, there is an *assumption* that the contributions of a full-time homemaker are equal in value to the contributions of a full-time wage earner.

Most states now recognize the value of homemaker services. The longer the marriage, the more likely it is that the economic contribution of a major wage earner and a homemaker will be found to be equal. However, women in dual income families do not receive credit for "double duty," even if they do most of the cooking, cleaning and caregiving.

- **Contribution to family expenses from non-marital sources**
  This is a factor that may be considered at the property division stage and may result in a reimbursement to the contributing spouse. An example of this kind of contribution is if you supported your husband while he went back to school. In most states, this factor would be considered at the property division stage of your divorce proceedings. The final decision would take into account the duration of your marriage and the length of time between earning the degree and when the divorce action began.

- **Duration of the marriage**
  This is one of the most important variables affecting the weight given both direct and indirect contributions to your marriage and its assets. As the length of the marriage increases, the source of the acquisition of assets is less important and greater weight is given to non-economic contributions, such as the role of the homemaker. The longer the marriage, the more equal the contribution is assumed to be. On the other hand, in a short-term marriage, direct financial contribution assumes a decisive role.

- **Future financial need**
  This is one of several factors has no basis in partnership theory, but reflects the public policy acknowledging the value that society places on families, childrearing and homemaking. It is the most important of the factors that are in this category.
  Future need of the spouses is a factor considered at the property division stage and may result in awarding a dependent spouse a

higher percentage of the marital assets. Duration of the marriage is again an important variable. In short-term marriages, future financial need is not as substantial a factor. In longerterm marriages, however, it is a vital factor for a dependent spouse.

- **Income**

  Income is a factor that is especially important if there is a disparity between the spouses. An underemployed or dependent spouse may be unable to meet future needs. The trial court may address this inequity by awarding a higher percent of property to the dependent spouse. In some states, a maintenance payment may be ordered to help strike a balance.

- **Standard of living established during the marriage**

  Standard of living during the marriage is a factor that serves as a benchmark for future financial needs. Duration of the marriage will influence the weight given to the standard of living as well. The longer the duration, the more likely that an arrangement will be created that helps to balance the situation. This factor is easily proved with documents of expenses, and easily refuted in the absence of such documents.

- **Assets, liabilities and non-marital assets**

  Anticipated income produced by assets and the ability to meet debt obligations are important factors affecting future financial needs. Health and age are two additional variables that have a bearing on future needs. Ability to replace assets, employability, future income-producing capacity and educational degrees are all elements of meeting future needs and will be considered.

  Some states include non-marital assets in the base figure, and others exclude them and instead weight them in the division of assets. Just because it is a non-marital asset, doesn't mean it doesn't count.

- **Enhanced earning capacity** (one spouse has increased their income-earning capacity during the marriage by higher education, training, or experience)

  New York is the only state to classify certain enhanced earning capacity as marital property. In other states, it is treated as a *factor to be considered* at the property division stage. In a traditional marriage, enhanced earning capacity may be the most valuable asset remaining following a divorce. A calculation establishing the economic value of that enhanced earning capacity provides the trial court with a guidepost to balance the inequity that may otherwise occur.

The reverse of enhanced earning capacity is opportunity cost. The loss of market wages and employment benefits, in addition to depreciated earning capacity, are economic factors that can be quantified. Without consideration of the opportunity costs to an under-employed or dependent spouse, the possibility that the spouse who earns a higher wage will realize an unjust enrichment increases.

- **Tax consequences**
  Most states recognize tax consequences as relevant if a taxable event is likely to occur at or shortly after divorce, and if the tax liability is easily calculated. The trial court will not consider speculative taxable events likely to occur sometime in the near future. Negotiated, mediated, and mutually agreed upon property settlements should take into account the tax consequences whether or not the trial court will make an allowance for that future tax obligation.

- **Custodial arrangements**
  Custodial arrangements and the needs of minor children are relevant factors in most states. Awarding a marital home to a custodial parent may be given more weight. There is some overlap between considering the needs of children at the property division state and establishing child support obligations.

A catchall factor is included in the statutes of a few states. This allows the trial court to consider any fact that is relevant. However, the express factors in most states are so broad that it is seldom necessary to use the catchall factor.

What You Need to do to Prove Your Case

Remember that you cannot expect to get a fair and equitable settlement without *proving* that you deserve it *under the law. The burden of proof is on you; do not expect the legal system to protect you!*

Once you and your team of professionals have identified all of the relevant factors in your situation, each factor needs to be quantified so that a trial judge (and the other side) can see your side of the case and weigh the factors based on the reality of the numbers.

You should be able to *prove*:

- What you and your spouse own and owe
- The value of everything
- What your standard of living was prior to the breakdown of the marriage
- Your future needs
- Special needs of children, health needs, educational needs
- Your ability to earn a living and provide for your future
- Tax consequences
- The relative economic comparison between you and your spouse that could include the change in standard of living
- How each of you will fare following the divorce

The factors relevant to your case should be summarized on one or two pages and then backed up with detailed economic analysis. Keep in mind that trial judges are usually overworked, underpaid and hear horror stories everyday. Your story should be told in numbers that are factual and unemotional.

List Your Assets and Liabilities

The next step in organizing your financial information is to begin to identify all of the property that either of you own, and all of the debts that either of you owe. Using the documents you have gathered, make a list of:

- The real estate you own, individually and together
  - » your primary place of residence
  - » vacation home
  - » investment or income-producing property
- All of the bank accounts that are in your names (individually and together)
  - » checking accounts
  - » savings accounts
  - » money market accounts
  - » CDs
  - » credit union accounts
- Brokerage accounts
- Mutual fund investments
- Individual stocks and bonds (note the number of shares and the values as of the latest date you have available)
- Businesses you or your husband own, even if you do not know

how much they are worth
- Partnerships in law, accounting, medical practice, etc.
- IRAs and pension plans
- Stock options and deferred income
- In New York, professional degrees, licenses and professional careers may be counted as a marital asset. Your attorney will guide you in determining the classification as to whether it is an asset or a factor.

Quantify Your Assets and Liabilities

Placing a value on some assets is an easy job. A bank statement, CD, or 401(k) contribution plan has a number and that is the value (although the value may fluctuate, it is what it is). On the other hand, putting a value on your house, other real estate, or a business or professional practice is a much more difficult task. Experts may be needed to prepare valuations for these assets. You may need to hire a CPA or a business evaluator who is an expert in business valuations to perform this job. Depending on the complexity of the financial situation, other experts may be brought in to assist.

Quantifying debts is a similar process. It is normal for mortgages to go with the house they are paying for, car loans to go with the car they are for, etc. Some difficulty occurs when there is disagreement as to who incurred the debt and if there is a dispute as to the use of the proceeds of the loans. Sometimes there are loans that one person applied for and was approved for with the other person having no knowledge of the loan. Unfortunately, just because you may not have approved of a loan, doesn't mean that it will not be considered a marital debt.

It's All About the Numbers

In some divorce cases, considerable time, money and emotional energy are spent on legal filings, emergency motions and legal rhetoric. As you may have noticed from my discussion so far, all of that time, money and energy will culminate in settlement that centers on one thing: money. Whether it is in the form of cash, a house, stock options, or a pension plan, it is all about who gets what.

Property vs. Maintenance

In the late 1970s and early 1980s, the courts were likely to award more property to dependent spouses rather than awarding them maintenance. This was based on two major considerations: 1) the possibility that the maintenance payments would be unenforceable and 2) the desire to sever all ties between the parties and allow them to plan for their futures without the burden of ongoing obligations to their former spouse.

This theory may be noble, but in the real world most divorcing couples do not have enough property to divide that will offset the value of a stream of income into the future.

The major asset a spouse walks away from a marriage with is their ability to earn a living. The financial reality for the homemaker is the decline in their standard of living, especially for long-term homemakers and mothers with small children. A disproportionate division of 55%, 60%, or 65% of property to a dependent spouse was not enough to offset the long-term benefit of the earning capacity of a major wage earner.

Later, in the mid-1980s, many states favored what was known as *rehabilitative maintenance.* Underemployed or unemployed homemakers were awarded maintenance for a defined period of time, perhaps three to five years, with the anticipation that they had an affirmative duty to seek training, education and a job. This also was a great theory, but in reality women who have been out of the workforce for years do not walk into jobs that pay well.

Currently, in the beginning of the third millennium, maintenance is being revived and expanded in many states. In recent years new statutes have established guidelines for the awarding of maintenance to a dependent spouse, especially in long-term marriages. The trend has been to consider more factors in structuring awards.

Conditions of Maintenance

In some cases, permanent maintenance is awarded, but it usually has conditions. The trial court will make awards for a period of three to five years with the court stipulating that it is maintaining jurisdiction and allowing for the review of the maintenance award. This functions to give the dependent spouse some protection.

In agreed settlements that do not go to trial, the negotiations cover not only the amount of the award and the length of time the award will remain in effect, but they often include discussion about conditions such as *reviewable, nonreviewable, modifiable* and *non-modifiable*.

If an award of maintenance is *reviewable*, the court has granted one of the parties the right to petition the court for a review of the need for maintenance at the end of a specified period. A dependent spouse would want to secure this right, while a payer spouse would not. It is sometimes possible to negotiate a high dollar amount and a long period by giving up the right to a *reviewable* award. If you are advised to do so, be cautious and make sure it is a fair trade-off.

A maintenance award that is *modifiable* gives each of the parties the right to petition the court to adjust the amount of the award, based on a change of circumstances. This might occur when a wage earner has fluctuating income or is in a position of increasing income.

A word of warning: Insist that your attorney explain all the legal terms of maintenance and have your financial planner calculate the dollar value of each option so you are making an informed decision.

Child Support Guidelines

The third element to your settlement, if you have minor children, is the kind and amount of child support you will be awarded. In the late 1980s the federal government initiated changes in the way child support was handled. Studies pointed to the lack of a uniform method for calculating child support obligations and the inability to enforce the payment.

The U.S. Department of Health and Human Services formed a committee to make recommendations. This committee relied on two major studies to establish measures on the cost of raising children: the U.S. Department of Agriculture's *Cost of Raising Children* and Dr. Thomas Espenshade's research, *Investing in Children*. Both studies focused on the additional cost of housing, food and transportation, along with direct, out-of-pocket expenses such as clothing, schooling, etc., that constituted the cost of raising children.

The committee explored a variety of formulas to assess an appropriate dollar amount to meet these needs. The federal government mandated that each state must have guidelines in place by October of 1989. Each state adopted guidelines that routinely applied per the formula that is in place within the state. All of the state's formulas factor in the income of payer and number of children in calculating the amount of the obligation by one or both of the parents.

In most cases the guideline amount has the status of *rebuttable presumption*. This simply means that it is presumed that the guideline amount is correct and just, and will be used *unless disputed by one of the parties*. For the court to grant a child support award that deviates from the guidelines, the judge must state the reason for the deviation in writing.

To justify a deviation from the guideline child support award, most states have a list of factors that would qualify for consideration. The factors include special needs, such as health or education, and standard of living. If you believe that your situation is special, the onus is on you to prove your case to the court.

Don't Forget About Health Insurance

COBRA is the acronym for the federal law passed in 1986 that requires companies that meet certain size limits to provide health insurance to the dependent spouse for a period of three years following a divorce from the covered employee. The dependent spouse will be the new policyholder and is expected to pay the premiums. This law was a remedy to the plight of women who could not get health insurance on their own following a divorce due to pre-existing health conditions.

Many states have enacted similar laws to cover companies that fall under the size limits set by the federal law. Some states also have insurance "pools" to cover those who would not otherwise qualify for health insurance.

Your Property Settlement:
Be careful what you ask for . . .

When considering assets such as stock options, investments, IRAs and even homes, don't assume that getting them is always better than not. There are many details regarding the transfer of ownership of these assets that you must fully understand in order to make the most informed decision. For instance, some assets have a built-in tax liability. Others are best transferred before the divorce rather than after it. Finding a financial planner who is an expert in divorce is a necessary part of your approach to your divorce because part of her job is to be up to date on all of the changes in tax law and all of the ways your choices now will affect your life in the future.

In my experience, there are several common problem areas during negotiations for property settlements. They are:

Imputed Income

Some business owners, executives, independent contractors, sole proprietors, and anyone who receives cash or tip income, could be adding substantially to the family's standard of living through perks and unreported income. If this is not calculated and included in the income available to pay maintenance and/or child support, a dependent family will be short-changed.

If this is an issue or you suspect that it might be, alert your attorney and financial planner early in the process. Your attorney may need to demand records to prove the values.

Keeping or Selling the House

Most marriages that have lasted at least five to ten years have acquired a home. In the past, especially in more traditional marriages where the wife was the homemaker and caregiver, it was the norm for the house to be awarded to the wife. This was a good news bad news situation. The good news was that women were being awarded the one asset that emotionally meant the most to them. But the bad news was that they usually did not have the financial income to maintain that asset. This was a major contributing factor to the decline in the standard of living for women.

Before agreeing to accept the house on your side of the ledger in the property division, I recommend calculating its long-term economic impact. Whether you are a long-term homemaker, a mother with young children, or a wage earner, you don't want to be surprised after the divorce is over by the financial reality of your property division. It could turn what was meant to be an equitable distribution into a financial burden.

When contemplating whether it is a good idea for you to keep the house, the most important consideration is the cash flow part of the equation. Make sure there will be enough money coming in to cover all of your expenses, including the mortgage, real estate taxes, assessments, homeowner insurance, and repairs and maintenance. Determine the terms of the existing mortgage and make sure the lender will allow you to assume the mortgage on your own. (And be careful not to take over a mortgage with a balloon payment due in one or two years unless you *know* that you will qualify to re-mortgage.)

In longer-term marriages, it is typical that the home was purchased years ago and perhaps was not the first home you own. In these cases the Taxpayer Relief Act of 1997, which provided substantial relief for divorcing couple, states that you are permitted up to a $250,000 exclusion (if you are filing individually) from capital gains tax from the sale of your principal residence (meaning you resided there for at least two of the five years prior to the sale).

This corrects a major problem for divorcing individuals who have moved out of the principal residence and who still had an ownership interest in the home. Before this tax law change, the home had to be the principal residence *at the time of the sale*. Therefore, the non-occupying individual is able to exclude $250,000 of gain when the house is sold even though that person did not actually occupy the house for two of the last five years before the sale.

The important message is to get professional help in assessing your situation and ascertaining which strategies might be appropriate for you. Call the IRS or go to their web site and get a copy of IRS Publication 523: Selling your Home, for all of the technical details affecting this part of your settlement.

Splitting the Pension

There are two main types of pensions: defined benefit and defined contribution. If your settlement involves a pension, obtain a copy of all of the paperwork as soon as possible.

In general terms, defined benefit pensions will pay a benefit at retirement based on a formula, such as years of service and average wages for a specific number of years, paid out for differing periods of time. *Defined benefit* pensions are usually *paid for by the employer. Defined contribution* pension plans are pension accounts held in the name of the individual wage earner and are accumulated from *volunteered contributions from the wage earner*, and perhaps also contributions from the employer.

There are an infinite variety and combination of pension plans, profit-sharing plans, employee savings plans, stock ownership plans, etc. There are a few important differences and opportunities with each major type of plan. Call the IRS or go to their web site and ask for a copy of IRS Publication 575: Pension and Annuity Income, for all of the technical details.

- **Value of the Plans**

  Defined contribution plans (of all kinds) have a value that is reported to the employee (or owner of the pension) at regular intervals and it is what it is. Defined benefit plans are benefits that will be payable sometime in the future and the value in today's dollars must be calculated to a "present value." If it is likely that you will be going to trial, discuss with your team of advisors the possibility of hiring an actuary to provide this calculation for you. (An actuary is a trained specialist who works n the area of pensions and annuities.)

  With the passage of federal legislation (Omnibus Reconciliation Act of 1986), most pensions can be transferred to an alternate payee (the spouse who is not the person who owns the pension) as a result of a divorce. This legislation was intended to remedy the inequities caused by the fact that under prior law, pensions could not be divided (and to this day there are still some pension plans that are not subject to division at divorce, such as those of local municipal employees). This inequity left many dependent spouses in long-term marriages with no pension benefits, even when those benefits had been earned during the marriage.

  The procedure for transferring pension benefits involves correctly completing a Qualified Domestic Relations Order (QDRO) once your divorce and property settlement have been granted. This form states that you are an alternate payee of the pension plan. The QDRO must be signed by the court and accepted by the administrator and/or custodian of the pension plan to enable the administrator of the pension to transfer your award to you. I usually ask the administrator for a prototype of a QDRO ahead of time to make certain it is in acceptable form.

  So if your husband has a 401(k) pension and profit-sharing plan, you can receive some or all of the money in the plan as part of the settlement in the divorce. Many plans allow the money to be transferred directly into a rollover IRA in your name and invested for her future, so that when you are 59½ you can begin drawing out money to live on.

- **Defined benefit plans are ordinarily not available for transfer.**

  Remember, this type of plan gives the pensioner a monthly payment based on a formula and it works like an annuity. However, an alternate payee (wife of the wage earner) can receive part or all of this future benefit, as long as:

» it is a part of the divorce settlement agreement *and*

» a QDRO has been approved by the court *and*

» the QDRO has been filed with and accepted by the administrator of the plan *and*

» the benefit granted to the alternate payee is not more than what the participant would have gotten. In other words, the alternate payee cannot be given a benefit that is not allowed under the plan documents.

Warning: It is essential that you and your team get copies of the pension plan documents that will spell out the parameters and rights under the plan.

- **Splitting the IRA or SEP**
  The splitting of an IRA or a SEP does not require a QDRO. A letter of transfer signed by both the owner of the IRA or SEP and the alternate payee will be sufficient, as long as the transfer is included as part of the property settlement. Any money rolled over into the payee's IRA continues to grow tax-deferred. The only time there is a taxable event, is if the rollover occurs *before* the divorce. If you do not wait until the divorce property settlement, the funds transferred to the alternate payee are considered a taxable distribution to the owner of the account.

Dirty Tricks

Because dirty tricks are so prevalent in divorces that go to trial, I feel compelled to tell you about some that I have seen over the years. Dirty tricks range from simple and annoying to devious and criminal. Regardless of their severity, the more you know about them, the more likely you will be to spot them if they are present in your situation. Remember that he wouldn't be doing anything underhanded if he weren't benefiting from it. And if he is benefiting, it is probably at your expense.

For example: A wage earner with W-2 income walks into his employer and asks the employer to begin withholding more federal and state taxes. The net income on his paycheck is less, and if his state calculates child support on net income, his child support payments will be less than they should be. In addition, he will receive a refund from the government for the overpayment of taxes.

Your attorney should protect you from any such scheme. But no one has more at stake than you do. It is in your best interest to be an active participant in your divorce action, and that means knowing as much about financial issues relating to your case as possible. Other common dirty tricks are:

- Income decreases in the year of the divorce (particularly for the self-employed, salespeople, commodity traders and small business owners).
- Loans to friends and/or relatives (this is known as "parking," and is then repaid after the divorce).
- Borrowing from the marital estate to pay off debts of the business (wife gets the house, with a large mortgage or line of credit, and the husband gets a debt-free business).
- Hiding assets (putting money or investments in others' names, putting cash in a safe deposit box, using offshore trusts, purchasing treasury bonds where the interest will not show up until the bonds are redeemed, or investing in deferred annuities that do not report interest that would show up on a tax return).
- Lost documents (when asked to supply documents, they are nowhere to be found).
- No money for dependent family (without a written order for temporary support, the wage earning spouse stops paying the mortgage or the utilities, or stops providing enough for everyday living expenses), which causes the dependent spouse to settle for a property and maintenance and/or child support agreement that is less than fair, but without funds she is unable to carry on the fight.
- Threat of custody battle. As father's rights have become more prevalent, the number of cases of fathers asserting to the court that they are the better parent has increased.

Warning: Do not expect the court to protect you. Know the limitation of the legal system.

It's Not Over Yet

Regardless of the method you have used to settle the financial issues, your divorce is not over until you have, in your own name, what has been awarded to you.

Once you have what is legally yours, you need to think about whom you want on your new, post-divorce support team and you need to learn about how to take care of your own personal finances.

Changing Titles and Beneficiaries

Assets, such as the house, will need to be transferred by re-titling the asset in your name. Other assets, such as bank accounts, brokerage accounts and IRAs, can be transferred by executing a letter of transfer with signature guarantees by a bank officer. In some instances, you may be asked to supply a copy of the divorce decree to the financial institution. Life insurance companies and custodians for IRAs and pension plans must be notified of beneficiary changes. If you and your husband had a will or a trust, you will need to make changes there, as well.

Make a list of all of the assets. List all of the companies and financial institutions and their phone numbers. Then, call all of them and ask what must be done to make the necessary changes. Write all of the letters, get all of the signature guarantees (usually both you and your husband will need to sign), and send off all the letters. Keep records if all letters and calls, and follow up until changes are completed.

Warning: Do not assume that your attorney will do this for you. Once the divorce is over, your divorce attorney will be off to put out the next fire on a pressing case. No one cares as much about your financial future as you do. If your attorney does handle this for you, expect to pay extra; it takes a lot of time, and time is money. Your financial planner can assist you with all of the transfers. Be sure to discuss fees and arrangements first.

Out With the Old . . . Advisors

If you and your ex-husband shared advisors (e.g., estate attorney, CPA, broker, insurance agent, banker, financial planner) prior to the breakdown of the marriage, now may be the time to assess which, if any of these advisors, you wish to continue to work with. Pursue a new advisor in the same systematic manner with which you chose your divorce attorney. Know your own needs and standards, and find advisors who you feel can best help you. Don't forget to ask how they expect to be compensated.

Filing Tax Returns

Your first order of business, if you are to receive taxable maintenance, is to start filing quarterly tax returns. Unless you are familiar with filing your own tax returns, find a CPA to calculate your quarterly payments and then help you organize your record keeping for filing annual federal and state income tax returns. You could also use an "enrolled agent" for this part of your process. Enrolled agents are individuals who have passed a series of exams on taxes, have the necessary educational requirements, and who are qualified to practice before the IRS in tax matters.

Adjusting to a New Standard of Living

Most women are likely to have to adjust to a lower standard of living as a result of their divorce. If you were not the spouse who paid the bills and monitored the investments, you should use this opportunity to learn as much as you can about personal finance. If you have a computer or can buy one, this is a good time to get used to using a money management software program to record all of your financial activity. It will take a small investment of your time to learn how to use the software, but it will pay off.

When you record all of your financial activity, it will be easy to see how much you spend, what your current net worth is and what expenditures affect your taxes. And if you find yourself back in court, as often happens in child support and maintenance disputes, you will have a record of income, maintenance received, child support payments and the cost of raising your children. At the very least, you will feel empowered because you will be in charge and in control of your spending choices.

Investing for the Rest of Your Life

Women who receive lump sum payments as part of their divorce settlements are often tempted to reward themselves with expensive trips, clothing and jewelry once the ordeal is over. Resist this temptation until you are certain that you can afford what you desire to purchase. Also resist making investments that sound too good to be true—they usually are! My advice is to make no investment decisions initially and keep your money in a money market or in CDs. These investment vehicles are safe, and while they won't make you a bundle, they are better than making hasty and unwise decisions that could cause you to lose your new money.

Now that the divorce is over, read and learn about your investment choices. Attend seminars sponsored by banks, brokerage firms, financial planners and mutual fund companies. Interview different types of advisors. Assess your needs and then choose an advisor that suits your style and makes you feel at ease.

Warning: Be careful out there! Beware of hot tips from your brother-in-law who just changed jobs or your well-meaning father and sister who want to protect you. Steer clear of relatives who want to borrow $10,000 to start a new business and anyone who wants to give you investment advice. Some advice is worth listening to, but know enough about investing to know what is good for you, and then make up your own mind.

Conclusion

Women have stayed home to raise children, have interrupted their own educations to put their husband's through college, have taken less demanding jobs to be able to spend more time at home, and have moved from location to location with a husband who was moving up the career ladder. Women have made those decisions based on the expectation that their husband would provide financial security. However, it is at divorce that most women are brought face-to-face with the reality of the financial cost to them for these lifestyle decisions.

Letting Go

For each of us, the letting go may be different. Emotions have been generated by the divorce itself: anger, resentment, frustration, disappointment, failure, fear and anxiety. Emotions relating to dreams not realized, planned trips not taken, joint pride in children not shared, loss of identity. And while it is certainly true that there are victims of the divorce process, victim is not a viable career choice. Some of the most exciting, successful and interesting women today are divorced. In many cases, they re-invent themselves after shedding their old identity. Some choose new careers, some choose to volunteer and some choose a life of philanthropy. You can too.

New Beginnings

Divorce is one of the most difficult life passages. But once it is behind you, sort through the ashes and put together the embers of a new beginning. For each of you, the path will be different. Fashion a life that is meaningful and uniquely your own. Make it your goal to get yourself into a position where you can choose the lifestyle you desire, and *you* can maintain it comfortably. And when you have a financial question, ask your expert. Take comfort in the fact that you so not have to be alone on the path to financial security. Enjoy your trip.

Chapter Six

Widowhood

By Cicily Maton, CFP™

The loss of a spouse can be your life's most traumatic, wrenching experience. Very few women are prepared to face all of the emotional, financial and social changes that rapidly occur upon the death of their husbands. If your husband has died there is a lot that you need to do to make certain that you are taking care of yourself. None of it is fun, but most of it is absolutely necessary to prepare yourself for a life of financial independence.

In this chapter, I will explain your non-negotiable tasks, such as dealing with probate if your husband had a will, as well as the choices you may be faced with, such as whether or not to sell your house. I will provide you with some structure at a time when you might be in desperate need of a list of things to do in order to feel any sense of accomplishment. In my experience, the grieving process can be so overwhelming and all encompassing that you can easily forget what day it is or whether you paid your mortgage. Your mental health and financial well-being will both benefit if you are able to take care of yourself and even be productive at a time when it is easy to think of nothing but pain. This financial passage—from couplehood back to single-hood—is involuntary. But how you come out of it is up to you . . .

Widowhood Often Leads to Poverty

Though grieving is a healing process that cannot be rushed, it must be tamed so that it doesn't ruin you financially. For many women, becoming a widow creates emotional upheaval, which in turn causes financial upheaval. If your husband was the person who handled all of the financial matters and all of the record keeping, it can be particularly difficult because you are faced with the need to educate yourself. Many women decide—consciously or otherwise—that grieving is far more important than financial literacy. Don't become one of those women.

According to the General Accounting Office, 80% of women living in poverty were not poor before their husbands died. There are several possible causes of this phenomenon. Two of the most common are that the women didn't work and/or they were not involved in the book-keeping and financial decisions of their family. If either or both are true for you, the good news is that you can educate yourself to financial literacy and find a financial planner whom you like and trust.

I am here to tell you that learning about financial matters and taking control over your financial life is not an option; it's a necessity. And your education should begin immediately, as the longer you wait, the more reasons you will create to avoid taking responsibility.

What to do Immediately

The most important thing you can do for yourself is to build a support system. Whether you go to gatherings of widows, speak with a grief counselor, or spend hours on the Internet chatting and leaving messages on message boards, you must do something to deal with your emotional state. Your emotional state is closely related to your ability to effectively handle your personal finances, so it is paramount that you deal with your grief, preferably with the help of an expert.

Grief manifests itself in all kinds of destructive ways when it is not properly dealt with. And some of those destructive ways can cost you a lot of money—and your future financial security.

> Kate and Fred were high school sweethearts who went to college together and married shortly after they graduated. Throughout their 36-year marriage, Fred worked his way up the corporate ladder and Kate stayed home raising the children, keeping the house and entertaining Fred's colleagues. They had four daughters who ranged in age from 28-35 when Fred suffered a heart attack at the age of 58. He died shortly thereafter.
>
> Kate and her daughters were devastated by Fred's sudden death. None of them knew what to do, and all of them were afraid to ask anyone for help with the finances because they were embarrassed by their ignorance. Kate's daughters were

particularly embarrassed as they were all professionals and yet they were not financially literate (their husbands took care of everything financial). Kate's sons-in-law overwhelmed her with all kinds of advice and investment tips and all of their voices began to sound like unintelligible noise.

Kate began to hide from everyone. She spoke only to her daughters, rarely answered the phone, and didn't open her mail. She turned down all offers for help, except from Fred's financial advisor, whom she put in charge of everything because Fred liked him, trusted him, and worked with him for years.

Kate refused to see a grief counselor or attend even one support group session; she didn't need to share any grief because she didn't have any. She was completely numb.

Before I met Kate (her oldest daughter took it upon herself to do some research and find a financial planner for her mother), she had just sold the house that she and Fred lived in for almost 30 years. In addition, she had just started shopping. A lot.

Kate's story is not at all uncommon and there is much to be learned from it. Most important is the reality that is worth repeating: Your emotional state is intimately related to your financial state. Whatever your response to your husband's death is—even if you feel numb and you don't think that is a dramatic reaction—that response is bound to affect your finances.

There is a broad spectrum of emotions involved with the death of a spouse and I cannot possibly address every combination of emotions in this chapter. However, I can speak, in general terms, of what I have observed in my own practice.

Generally speaking, although there are many feelings that arise after the death of a spouse, if they directly affect your finances it is usually because you spend with less awareness. This can take the form of a shopping habit or giving money to charity. Whatever the rationalization is, the end result is that you manage to get rid of your money. Whether the reason is because you are numb, you are in desperate need of a distraction, you have just become wealthy due to the death of your husband, or you feel guilty, if you are spending like never before you could have a serious financial problem in a short period of time.

Another way you can relieve yourself of your money is by taking bad advice, following hot stock leads, funding your nephew's new business, or by giving your money to a broker, an insurance salesperson, or some other person who promises to quadruple it. There are unscrupulous people all over, and some go so far as to read obituaries and then target widows. There are very few financial decisions you *must* make immediately following your husband's death. Anyone who tells you that you have to "act now" is probably trying to exploit you financially.

And though you might not try to get rid of your money, you might try to rid yourself of things that remind you of your husband, such as your house (like Kate did). The natural response to extreme pain such as death is to want to get as far away from it as possible. But because your feelings are bound to evolve, selling your house could very well be a mistake. You might consider "seeing the seasons through" before making such a major decision.

Your Husband's Advisors

Another common phenomenon among widows, which Kate from the above story experienced, is a resistance to changing financial advisors. For example, upon reviewing Kate's financial records, it became clear that many bad investment decisions were made. Now, since Kate was not part of the management of the finances, it was unclear whether the bad decisions were Fred's, or whether they were based on bad advice from his advisor. Regardless, the result was not what I would call effective management of his portfolio.

If that weren't enough of a problem, Kate, like many widows, was attached to both Fred's investment choices and his investment advisor. This occurred for two reasons: because she didn't want to let go of anything related to her husband, and because she didn't want to come face to face with his inadequacies. In fact, she was devastated by the thought that he made a lot of expensive mistakes and bad decisions, and it took me months to get her to eliminate or reverse anything. And she desperately needed to because all of those decisions from the past—good or bad—were made based on a dramatically different reality. Kate's financial strategy as a widow is much different from when Fred was alive.

My advice to widows who were not involved in their finances is this: You are beginning a new cycle in your life, and you are in charge of it. This cycle is defined by becoming financially literate, hand-picking your team of expert advisors and finding support people who are going to help you create the best future possible for you.

Though there are not many financial decisions to be made during the time immediately following the death of your husband, there are definitely things to do that are *related* to your financial situation. The following list is not exhaustive—only your financial advisor will be able to tell you all of the tasks you need to tackle. But it is a solid beginning.

If you do not currently have a CERTIFIED FINANCIAL PLANNER™, I suggest you focus your search on locating one who specializes in the financial ramifications of widowhood. She will invariably be well acquainted with the emotional and social aspects, as well, so she will probably be a good source for other referrals (such as local support groups, therapists, lawyers and accountants).

However, be careful not to expect your financial planner to be all things to you just because she is knowledgeable about widowhood. Unless she is also a licensed, practicing therapist and lawyer, use your planner for financial issues and get emotional and legal help from the appropriate experts.

Get Organized

Grief is overwhelming for many women. And if that is the case for you, it is crucial that you understand that *you need to take care of yourself during your grieving process.* Taking care of yourself means everything from getting your hair cut to grocery shopping to paying your monthly bills. This is no time to neglect your bills and let your credit be harmed. If your husband was the person who performed any of the tasks necessary to maintain your lifestyle, then you need to learn how to do those things.

Begin by making a commitment to getting organized for your journey through your grief and into the next stage in your life. I suggest choosing a specific room or space just for the task of sorting through the piles of paperwork you have (or are going to have). An optimal space would have a telephone, perhaps a fax machine, a desk space, some file space, and it would also include a fireproof box (with a lock) for important documents. You will be making a to-do list from the items below for each week, so you can see a big picture. And each day, check the items on your list so you can see all of the progress you are making. When you are grieving a week is a long time, and that time is easily lost if you do not have a plan and some structure for your days.

Some of the things you need to collect for the space you are using to take care of business are your husband's:

• Personal papers, including his will and any other documents that state his wishes in the event of his death (such as how he

        would like to be buried)
- Personal telephone book
- Credit card statements
- Copies of bank and brokerage account statements
- IRA paperwork
- Documents from benefits such as 401(k), employee savings, profit-sharing plans, defined benefits and stock options
- Most recent pay stubs
- Tax records (including W-2 forms, 1099s and interest statements)
- Life insurance policies
- Homeowner's insurance policies
- Records of charitable contributions
- Health insurance records, if he paid for any or all of his premium
- Mortgage papers
- Limited partnership papers
- Employment contracts
- Records of current real estate investments, artwork, collectibles and antiques
- Records of any other investments for the past five years so you can determine exactly where your assets are and their assessed or estimated value

You won't be using all of these items immediately, but you will need them eventually. Locating them now and putting them in a safe, secure place may seem like busy work, but it is very important and it will help prepare you for their use. Keep a notebook to maintain a master list of the contents of your workspace, as well as a record of everything you are doing.

It may seem obvious, but the first thing you need to do is notify family, friends, employers, employees and business partners about your husband's death. Also contact his bank, credit card companies, insurance companies (including car insurance) and any other entities that he made a monthly payment to, and apprise them of his death. You will probably need to do this again, in writing, and perhaps include a death certificate. But for now, make the initial call to let them know you are taking control and ask them to explain precisely what you need to do next. *For all of your phone correspondence, record whom you spoke with and the date and time of the conversation.*

If your husband's death was work related or some kind of accident, you need to contact a lawyer immediately, as you may be entitled to workers' compensation benefits or have a legitimate claim for wrongful death.

Also ask creditors for any final bills and notify any institution that holds an account in both of your names to change it to your name alone. Assets, such as the house, will need to be transferred by re-titling the asset in your name. Other assets, bank accounts, brokerage accounts and IRAs, can be transferred by executing a letter of transfer with signatures guaranteed by a bank officer. Life insurance companies and custodians for IRAs and pension plans must be notified of beneficiary changes. If you and your husband had a will or a trust, you might need to make changes there, as well.

When you plan the funeral and burial, if they weren't planned in advance, be sure to shop around. The fact is that there are people who will try to take advantage of you because they know that you are grieving and vulnerable. The key to effective shopping is in making sure you are comparing apples to apples. Get itemized price estimates from each funeral home and cemetery, and carefully review them before you make a decision.

The decisions for the funeral and burial raise an important topic: your new budget. If your husband was employed and you do not know exactly what your husband's net income was each month, look at his pay stubs and find out. If your husband was retired and receiving a monthly pension, determine if that will continue or if there will be a reduced amount that you are entitled to. Add any other income he received each month (not including investment income) and you have his contribution to your monthly finances. You are not including investment income because that will continue. But the paychecks won't, so you need to create a new budget for yourself.

While you are creating that budget and preparing for the funeral and burial, remember to keep current with your monthly bills. It's easy to toss all of your mail into a pile every day, without even opening any of it. But as miserable as you feel, you can actually feel worse if you sabotage yourself by not doing what needs to be done.

Obtaining copies of your husband's death certificate is your next important task, and your funeral director should be able to help you. You are probably going to need many more copies than you could imagine. Think of it this way: Each person or entity that is a holder of any asset or debt account in your husband's name is going to need to verify his death with a copy of the death certificate. So the more accounts or individual entities that he was dealing with, on the asset side as well as the debt side, the more death certificates you are going to need.

Make a Budget

The absence of your husband will alter your day-to-day financial life. Whether or not you work, your money will be allocated differently and you will think about your future financial life differently, particularly if your husband was the breadwinner. In order to make a budget, you will have to determine how much income you will be getting, when you will get it and where it will come from. Then, you will need to establish how much you owe (and don't forget to include any tax obligations). After you subtract what you owe from what you have, what is the monthly number you are left with? That amount is what is going to have to get you from month-to-month. If you owe more than you have, you are going to have to omit some or all of your monthly "extras" (facials, massages, shopping, expensive dining out).

The fourth chapter of this book, Career and Retirement, explains how to determine exactly how much money you need each month (excluding unexpected emergencies). If you have never done this exercise, it is well worth it, as you should always know precisely where you are financially. As for your income, it may now come from a variety of places, including life insurance proceeds, Social Security, and whatever assets your husband transferred to you in his will or by trust.

The IRS

After the funeral and burial you will face the probate process if your husband had a will. Probate is when the will is read and any debts left by your husband are paid, including creditors and the fee for the executor of the estate. If you are the executrix of your husband's estate, you probably know there are some forms to fill out and file, with the IRS as well as with the state, as part of your duties. For instance, after the assets of the estate have been distributed to their intended beneficiaries, you must notify the IRS, in writing, that the estate has been "terminated" (you can use IRS form 56 for this purpose).

The IRS has publications that thoroughly explain how to complete the forms you will need to submit. Publication 559, for Survivors, Executors and Administrators contains a checklist of the forms you need and their due dates, a comprehensive example of what needs to be done, and a list of frequently asked questions. You can get it from your local IRS office or from www.irs.gov.

One of the forms you are going to have to file is a final return for your husband for whatever portion of the year he was alive. For this, you will need any W-2 forms, 1099 forms and statements of rental income and interest. The return is due the April after he passed away (the same time it would have been due if he were alive). You probably have a handle on his income, but don't forget about deductions, such as health insurance, charitable contributions, and business-related expenses.

I highly recommend enlisting the aid of a CPA or enrolled agent for this return and the subsequent estate tax return (and others) you must file. The estate tax return is a report you are making to the federal government that includes an inventory of all of the property that was owned solely by your husband. It ordinarily must be submitted to the IRS within nine months of the date of your husband's death (i.e., you can file for an extension).

As for *your* tax return, you have a choice in how you will file: either a joint return or separately. And if you have a dependent child at home, you may file a joint return for the subsequent two years, as well. Ask your accountant what the most beneficial strategy is for your unique circumstances.

Urgent: If Your Husband was an Owner or Partner . . .

If your husband was an owner or a partner in a business venture, you probably are going to have to make some important decisions. First, you must establish what type of business he had an interest in, according to the IRS. In other words, was it a corporation or a partnership? Locate the papers and ask your attorney to explain what you need to do, how you need to do it, and whether there are options available to you for how to proceed. Then, take all of that information to your financial planner and ask her to explain the financial implications of what you must do. If you have options, ask her to describe the financial implications of those, as well.

Life Insurance and Other Benefits

In most cases, after your husband's death has been verified, you will be required to file for any benefits that are now yours. This includes insurance claims. If you are not certain of all possible life insurance benefits that are due you, write to the American Council of Life Insurance, Policy Search Dept., 1001 Pennsylvania Ave., NW, Washington, DC 20004. Tell them you need a missing policy search form and they will explain what you need to do and how long it might take.

Locate your husband's policy information (or get it from the missing policy search), read it very carefully, and bring it to your financial planner, as there may be some decisions that you need to make, such as how to receive the proceeds (in a lump sum or an annuity). Each person's situation is different, so I cannot make a general recommendation here. What I can say is that your decision will be contingent upon your present income, your short-term future need, and your tax situation.

In addition, if your husband had more than one job during his work life, be sure to call all of his current and past employers and inquire about any retirement plan benefits he had accrued. You may have choices about how you will receive benefits from your husband's retirement plan. Again, your choice is ordinarily between a lump sum payout and an annuity. However, in some instances, if your husband hadn't already retired you are permitted to delay payment. Once again, there are several variables that will be factored into your decision, including your tax situation. Make sure your consult your financial planner as soon as possible; there might be a time limit within which you need to make your election.

Also ask about medical insurance, as well. If your health insurance was company-sponsored by your husband's employer, you probably will be covered for at least 18 months and perhaps up to three years. You can determine if you have coverage and how long it will last by thoroughly reading through your current policy, calling the insurance provider, or asking the benefits specialist from your husband's employer to explain where you stand. I suggest doing all three and making sure there is unanimous agreement about your status.

If you are entitled to keep the insurance through his employer (and pay the premiums), don't automatically do that without first comparing prices of policies you can purchase on your own. Shopping around can make a big difference. But don't take too long to shop, as you have 30 days to notify your husband's company of his death, and then 60 days to decide if you want the policy from his company.

Social Security

If you were married for at least nine months before your husband died, you are eligible for Social Security benefits (contact the Social Security Administration to file your claim at your local office, at 800-772-1213, or at www.ssa.gov).

- If you are widowed before your spouse's Social Security payments would have begun, you can receive a widow's benefit at age 60 (unless you are disabled, in which case you can collect as early as age 50). If you are widowed after Social Security payments have begun, and you were receiving spousal benefits, you will continue to receive the higher of the two benefits: yours or your husband's, but not both. In addition, if you choose to remarry, your benefits will continue. (Congress made that possible in 1984, after noting the number of seniors who were living together in order to maintain their benefits.)
- The amount of your monthly benefit depends on your age when you start collecting and the amount your husband was receiving, or was entitled to receive. The amount of your benefit ranges from 71½ percent of your husband's benefit amount if you begin receiving them at age 60, to 100 percent of the amount if you begin receiving them at 65.

There are several options and conditions for the widow's benefit you are entitled to, and you should speak with the Social Security department to determine exactly what you are eligible for. Armed with that information, go to your financial planner to establish whether there is a best option from a planning standpoint.

Adjusting to a New Standard of Living

Some women have to adjust to a lower standard of living as a result of their husband's death, but all widows will have a different lifestyle. If you were not the spouse who paid the bills and monitored the investments, you should use this opportunity to learn as much as you can about personal finance. If you have a computer or can buy one, this is a good time to get used to using a money management software program to record all of your financial activity. It will take a small investment of your time to learn how to use the software, but it will pay off.

When you record all of your financial activity, it will be easy to see how much you spend, what your current cash flow is and what expenditures effect your taxes.

Letting Go

For each of us, the letting go may be different. Emotions have been generated by the death itself: anger, resentment, frustration, sadness, disappointment, failure, fear, anxiety and even relief. Emotions relating to dreams not realized, planned trips not taken, joint pride in children not shared, loss of identity. In many cases, widows re-invent themselves after shedding their old identity. You can too.

New Beginnings

The loss of your husband is often devastating emotionally. Many widows find great comfort in seeking professional counseling. There are also support groups in every community and dozens of web sites and chat rooms dedicated to the myriad concerns of widows. My goal is to help you prevent subsequent financial devastation. I hope you share my goal. After you have "taken care of business," it is time to re-invest in yourself. After all, you are now a single woman, and you are free to choose your new path.

My Advice

Meet with your financial planner immediately to begin creating a financial plan for you as a single woman. Review your insurance needs, change your will and change the beneficiaries on any other policies where your husband was the beneficiary. Discuss your retirement needs. Go over your cash flow plan in detail to make certain you can cover your monthly expenses and you know where your money is coming from and when.

Remember that the average age of widows in America is 55. How old are you? Given your family history and your health, what is the average life expectancy for someone like you (your insurance company can tell you). Though you can never predict what will happen, you should create your financial plan to give you sufficient resources for a long life.

As for precisely what your plan will look like, I cannot give you detailed advice, as I do not know the particulars of your situation. The one thing I can advise every widow to do is to you keep your money in a money-market account for about a year and spend your time healing and thinking about your new life. Many women find it easy to spend large sums of money at this point in their lives because it makes them feel better for a moment. Whether they are spending because they miss their husbands, they are angry at their husbands for leaving them, or they are so numb that they don't even realize what they are doing, the result is the same: damage to their financial futures.

As far as what *not* to do with your money goes, the advice is universal: Don't make any large purchases or any investments. In addition, don't give control of your money to anyone, and don't let anyone tell you that you have to make *this* financial decision, *right now, or else.* As I have mentioned, there are very few financial decisions that absolutely cannot wait (such as how you will take retirement plan benefits or life insurance proceeds).

Let Your New Self Emerge

After you have met with your planner and your therapist (or support group) and you are doing what needs to be done, focus on your new self. Take the classes you always wanted to take, learn a second, third, or fourth language. Start a philanthropic foundation. Plan some future travel. Think about any and everything you want to do with your life and write it all down. And don't stop until you've created a plan to make each item on your wish list a reality.

Chapter Seven

Estate Planning

By Roberta Welsh, CFP™

Do you know what would happen to the things you own and the money and investments in your accounts if you passed away tomorrow?

Do you have a will?

Do you have a living will?

Do you have a medical directive or power of attorney?

Do you know what estate taxes are?

Do you have a plan for gifting your money and other assets while you are living in addition to after you die?

In other words, *do you have an estate plan, and if you do, when was the last time you reviewed it?*

Preparing for Estate Planning

There are entire books devoted solely to estate planning. Most are hundreds of pages long. Though purchasing one of those books certainly cannot hurt, the danger that can result is a do-it-yourself plan that may not accomplish your objectives. Think about it this way: I studied and practiced for 15 years before I could call myself an expert in estate planning. And I'm still studying and practicing, as the details and the rules of estate planning are constantly changing.

Estate planning is, for some people, the most complex part of their financial planning process. It is also the least understood. In this chapter, I will introduce you to the basics of estate planning and tell you what you can do *before* you go to your CERTIFIED FINANCIAL PLANNER™ practitioner. There are some things you should do on your own, as they will save you money and help you understand the factors that directly impact your estate planning and your current finances. On the other hand, there are some things you shouldn't do without the help of an experienced professional, as you could easily put your estate at risk. The best client is one who is aware of the details of her financial life, yet knows when she needs to enlist the aid of an expert.

The Reasons for a Good Estate Plan

Most people I know are not happy about the amount of income tax they have to pay. And as their taxes increase, so does their discontent. But for individuals whose net worth totals $675,000 in the year 2001, or for married couples whose total assets are valued at over $1,350,000, there is a much bigger problem: estate taxes.

The highest federal income tax bracket is 39.6%, but estate taxes can run as high as 55%! If you do not have a satisfactory estate plan in place when you die, your death could actually have a financial cost to your heirs in addition to an emotional cost.

Another problem that you can avoid for your heirs is probate. Probate can be costly and it can also delay the time it takes to transfer your assets to your heirs. And if you do not have all of the necessary elements in place, it is possible that someone else will decide where your money will go. Good estate planning makes the transfer of assets as seamless and as painless as possible, while also minimizing estate taxes.

The First Thing You Need to Do:
Write Down Everything You Have

Your entire estate planning process will hinge on one piece of information: How much your estate is worth. The reason for this is simple: if your gross estate is worth $675,000 or more, it will be assessed a tax. And due to the Taxpayer Relief Act of 1997, that number will rise to:

- $700,000 in 2002
- $850,000 in 2004
- $950,000 in 2005, and to
- $1,000,000 in 2006

If assets exceed these limits, the estate tax must be paid before your assets are distributed. Naturally, this will reduce the amount that your heirs will receive.

Fortunately, there are ways of minimizing the tax burden, but for now let's attend to your estate. If you do not have a current itemized list of your assets and liabilities, this is the time to complete one. Your financial planner will have a form that will help you do this. However, in order to maximize your time with your planner (particularly if she is compensated on an hourly basis), you should do your calculations prior to your meeting. Moreover, this is very important information that you need to know about your financial life.

Below is the assets and liabilities worksheet that I use with my clients. Your planner's may differ slightly. Before you begin, you should know that the value of any asset is its current market value, which could be nowhere near what you paid for it, either because of its appreciation or depreciation.

Furthermore, when you are looking for assets to include in your gross estate, don't forget the following:

- Whether the assets are individually owned or jointly owned.
- The primary and contingent beneficiaries you currently have on any accounts such as retirement, insurance or annuity assets.
- Tangible personal property such as cars, cash, stocks, bonds, clothing, art, jewelry and antiques.
- The death benefit of life insurance, both group life insurance and individually owned life insurance. This item is also included in your estate if you changed ownership within three years of your death.
- Real estate (also known as *real property*), less the mortgage.
- Intellectual property, such as copyrights and patents.
- Any assets held offshore (contrary to popular belief, you do not avoid all taxes on them).
- Qualified retirement plan proceeds.
- Business ventures.

CURRENT NET WORTH STATEMENT

	Client	Spouse	Joint
RESERVES			
Cash/Checking accounts	$_____	$_____	$_____
Money Market accounts	_____	_____	_____
Savings account	_____	_____	_____
Certificates of Deposit (CDs)	_____	_____	_____
Life Insurance cash value	_____	_____	_____
Life Insurance Death Benefit (Group)	_____	_____	_____
Life Insurance (Individually Owned)	_____	_____	_____
TOTAL RESERVES	_____	_____	_____
INVESTMENT ASSETS			
Stocks and bonds	$_____	$_____	$_____
Business interests	_____	_____	_____
Direct investments	_____	_____	_____
Mutual funds	_____	_____	_____
Investment real estate	_____	_____	_____
Retirement plans @ work:			
IRAs	_____	_____	_____
Roth IRAs	_____	_____	_____
TOTAL INVESTMENT ASSETS	_____	_____	_____
PERSONAL ASSETS			
Auto	$_____	$_____	$_____
Boats	_____	_____	_____
Furnishings	_____	_____	_____
Residence	_____	_____	_____
Second Home	_____	_____	_____
Real Estate-Other	_____	_____	_____
TOTAL PERSONAL ASSETS	_____	_____	_____
TOTAL ASSETS (A)	_____	_____	_____

LIABILITIES

Current bills	$_____	$_____	$_____
Bank and installment loans	_____	_____	_____
Insurance loans	_____	_____	_____
Mortgage on residence	_____	_____	_____
a. original—current	_____	_____	_____
b. % of interest	_____	_____	_____
c. years remaining	_____	_____	_____
Mortgage on second home	_____	_____	_____
a. original—current	_____	_____	_____
d. % of interest	_____	_____	_____
e. years remaining	_____	_____	_____
Mortgage on real estate (other)	_____	_____	_____
a. original—current	_____	_____	_____
b. % of interest	_____	_____	_____
c. years remaining	_____	_____	_____
Notes payable	_____	_____	_____
Potential capital gains tax Liabilities	_____	_____	_____
Endorsements or unsettled damage	_____	_____	_____
Other	_____	_____	_____
TOTAL LIABILITIES	_____	_____	_____
NET WORTH (A minus B)	$_____	$_____	$_____
TOTAL NET WORTH			$_____

As you see, your estate's value, according to the IRS, is the net value after you have subtracted your liabilities from your assets. If your estate is worth over $675,000 (single or $1,350,000 joint) in the year 2001, you have an estate tax situation to manage.

It's Not Just About Taxes

Although it may seem that estate planning is all about tax minimization, that is not the case. I began this chapter with that information because it is the deciding factor for how you will approach estate planning. If your estate is taxable, you simply have more to consider.

The parts of estate planning that you need to address, regardless of the size of your estate, are: developing objectives for the assets in your name at death, deciding who will be in charge of your assets if you should become incapacitated, and clarifying your wishes about life-sustaining medical treatment for yourself. Essentially, it all comes down to: Whom do you want to get what when you die, whose hands do you feel comfortable putting your assets in, and do you want to accept medical intervention to prolong your life.

These are the parts of financial planning that you should contemplate before you go to your planner. Your planner will help you with the details of how to best accomplish your objectives, but the objectives themselves are up to you.

Points to Ponder

When you contemplate your own mortality, you are likely to experience thoughts and emotions that are overwhelming. Some people imagine that the signing of their will is foreshadowing their imminent death! This is particularly common for people who do not have a good estate plan. A common scenario is: You are suddenly thinking about all of your assets and to whom you want them to go. If you know that you do not have written instructions that state your wishes in the proper way, you feel panic, imagining all of the ways you could die before your estate plan is finalized by your attorney.

Here are some things to think about:

- If you have a husband or partner, you probably want to make certain that person's standard of living is maintained. You can provide financial help for them and allow your assets to pass on to someone else, if you so desire. Also think about what else you want for your husband or partner, besides financial support. Make a list.

- If you have children or other dependents, what do you wish for them? Which assets might they appreciate from your estate? Your jewelry, cars, homes and other property will come to mind here, but also consider support for future homes, tuition and business ventures. See Chapter Three for more about estate planning for children with special needs.

- If you are leaving anything to children or grandchildren, think about the impact that inheritance could have on them. If your bequest is going to catapult them into a new tax bracket, they will probably need to orient themselves psychologically to the new money.

- What are your favorite charitable causes and would you like to remember them in your will? The following chapter on Philanthropy will provide you with details as to the best way to handle this aspect of your financial plan.

What Everyone Needs to Know

The vocabulary of estate planning contains many terms that the layperson may think she understands. In my experience, many people do not have a satisfactory grasp of the basic language and some briefing (or tutoring) is usually necessary. There's nothing wrong with that; I recommend that you acquaint yourself with as much of the vocabulary as possible. Doing so will help your meetings with your planner cover the unique aspects of your estate plan rather than general definitions.

Let's begin by examining what is at the center of the estate planning process: the taxable estate.

The Taxable Estate

At the beginning of this chapter, I commented that estate planning is especially necessary for those whose estates are worth more than $675,000 (and I mentioned that that number is going to rise). This number, $675,000 is what is called the *unified credit*.

The federal government has stated that the first $675,000 worth of assets in your estate as an individual can pass to whomever you want it to upon your death—without any gift or estate tax assessed (more on gift tax in a moment). Therefore, you and your husband can each transfer up to $675,000 of assets before you reach the point where you will have to pay estate taxes.

The only exception is for gross estates of over $10 million. In their case, there is no $675,000 shelter for gifts *upon your death*, but there is for lifetime gifts (i.e., gifts transferred during your lifetime). Technically, the federal estate tax for estates over $10 million is a larger percentage than smaller estates (if the bequests are transferred upon your death).

So how exactly is it that you will pay all of these taxes if you are deceased, anyway? Any Living Trust, beneficiary designation, or your will can outline your wishes for who will inherit what. But the estate tax will be paid from your estate, either by borrowing the money or by selling assets is the cash is not available. This is when life insurance proceeds offer liquid assets (cash) to pay the estate taxes. I'll begin by discussing the tool that you probably are familiar with: the will.

The Will

Your will is the document that explains who gets what when you die and names someone to carry out your wishes. That person is called the executrix (or executor, if male) and you should discuss your decision with that person before you write your will. Many people consider the position to be a difficult and time-consuming one, and would rather not be named executrix. If you have any reason to believe that those who survive you might become at all contentious at the reading of your will, you should choose the person most willing and able to handle that situation. You should also name a successor executrix, in the event that your original choice is not able to fulfill the necessary duties.

Your will is drafted by an attorney and then notarized, and the original should be kept in a safe place, perhaps with your attorney. (Contrary to popular belief, a handwritten will is not just as good, and in fact is not recognized by all states.) You should keep copies in your safe deposit box and in a safe place in your home and you should reveal the location to someone you trust. Ask your attorney whether the original may be kept in your safe deposit box. In some states the safe deposit box is sealed at death, and it takes time and money to release it.

If you do not currently have a will you should have one drafted immediately because if you die without a will (i.e., *intestate*) all of your assets will be distributed according to state law (i.e., laws of intestacy), in which case your wishes may not be fulfilled. If you are not married and you would like to leave your property to your life partner (male or female), you must have a will that describes your wishes, or you must own individual assets jointly (see **Ownership of Property**). In no state do the laws of intestacy say your property will go to your partner rather than your closest blood relatives.

Once the will is finalized, you need to double-check the primary and secondary beneficiaries on your retirement, insurance and similar assets. Those designations override the will, i.e., such items will pass to whomever you have specified in the beneficiary designations. The goal is to make your asset titling and beneficiary items consistent with your new will.

Upon your death, your executrix must file a Petition for Probate of Will and Appointment of Executor in the county of your legal residence. Your executrix is then named publicly and the process of *probate* begins. *Probate* (which means "prove the will") is the judicial proceeding wherein your final debts are settled and the property in your will is formally passed to your heirs according to your instructions. It can be a time-consuming and expensive process (the national average is 6-10% of the value of the estate), and everything that occurs is a matter of public record. The expense of probate is less if you are using a family member rather than a professional executrix; the figure above usually includes an executrix fee plus probate tax and filing fees.

Before the assets subject to probate (described in your will) are transferred to their new owners, they must be collected and appraised. During this time, your executrix may have to publish legal notice in the newspaper that your estate is currently in probate. This functions to give creditors and anyone else the opportunity to stake their claim for an interest in your estate. They would make their requests in writing, to your executrix, who may need to hire an attorney to determine their validity.

Note the duties of your executrix and the importance that you choose a capable, levelheaded, and trustworthy person. And though the job may seem undesirable to some, you can provide for compensation through your will (e.g., a pre-determined percentage of the assets in the will, an hourly compensation, or a lump sum figure).

Among the debts that need to be settled could be: liabilities or debts accumulated during your lifetime, funeral expenses, legal fees, accounting fees, medical expenses and the fee for your executrix. If you have a sizable estate, the biggest chunk of your debt, however, will be payable to the IRS for your estate tax. And while it seems logical that the amount of estate tax you will have to pay depends on the value of your assets, that is not necessarily the case.

The reason for that is that *your* definition of ownership is not the same as the *IRS'* definition. The manner in which your assets are legally held is what determines whether, according to the IRS, they technically belong to you and to whom they should be transferred in the event of your death. Assets held jointly will automatically transfer to the joint owner. IRAs, profit-sharing plans and life insurance policies will automatically pass to the beneficiary that you have named. And any assets owned by a trust will follow the directive of the trust agreement. So any other assets held in your name individually will pass through probate according to your will (see **Ownership of Property**).

There is another type of will, one that articulates your desires in the event that you become incapacitated, and it is called the *living will.*

The Living Will

A living will is a legal document that explains your wishes in the event that you are incapacitated and will need the aid of artificial life support equipment in order to remain alive. It also addresses when you would like treatment to cease if you have a terminal illness. The living will allows you to dictate what will occur in this circumstance, and your family, loved ones, and physicians and other healthcare practitioners must abide by your wishes. Your attorney can keep your original living will and you should give a copy to your physician to keep in your file, and keep another copy at home with your other personal documents.

Durable Powers of Attorney

Durable powers of attorney name at least one person who will make decisions for you if you become incapacitated. These powers of attorney cover medical issues as well as issues pertaining to your assets.

The Durable Power of Attorney/Medical Directive

The durable power of attorney is a legal document that states that you are naming one or more people to manage your affairs, on your behalf, if you become incapacitated. Your affairs include the management of your finances as well as decisions over your healthcare. The management of your finances includes paying income taxes while you are alive, and then estate taxes when you die. It can also include the management of your business.

This document, which is created by an attorney, is flexible and can be customized to suit your needs. For instance, if you would prefer that your business partner manage your shared business in the event of your incapacitation, but you want your life partner to manage your finances, you can state that explicitly. As long as this document is properly drafted, it is legally binding and your loved ones and your medical practitioners must abide by it. Your attorney can keep the original, the person whom you are appointing should have a copy, and you should keep a copy in your home with your other personal documents.

The Durable Healthcare Power of Attorney/Medical Directive
(some states combine the two)

The durable healthcare power of attorney is a legal document that names the person whom you would like to make medical decisions for you if you become unable to make those decisions yourself. In the document, you describe any specific wishes you have, and you give the appointed person the authority to make decisions that are in your best interest.

This power of attorney is not recognized in all states and you should consult your planner about whether it is appropriate for you. It may be possible to add language to cover the use of the document when traveling or if you are in another state when medical decisions must be made. And if that clause is appropriate, you should make certain it is properly drafted and includes all of your wishes, explained as specifically as possible. Your attorney can keep the original, the person you are appointing should have a copy, and you should keep a copy at home with your other personal documents.

Trusts

A trust is a document that allows a person or an institution to hold the legal title to your personal property. It is a private agreement between you and another person that will allow for the distribution of specified assets to the beneficiaries of your choice, in the manner you have chosen. For instance, if you wanted to give your child a $1 million inheritance, and you wanted to provide a system for the distribution of those funds so the child couldn't have free access to it, the best way to do that would be to create a trust with the child named as a beneficiary.

There are several reasons why many financial planners and attorneys recommend trusts. Primarily, trusts offer flexibility. For instance, you have the option of transferring *ownership* of assets to the trust, or simply *title*. So if you have some assets of great worth that you don't want to be included in your taxable estate, you can transfer their ownership to an irrevocable trust, and bequeath from there. An irrevocable trust, as the name suggests, cannot be revoked. Consequently, there can be some significant gift tax issues in creating irrevocable trusts, so this needs to be reviewed ahead of time.

Trusts are far more than instruments of tax management, however. They are also instruments that permit you to help your heirs protect their bequests. Let's take the example of that $1 million you wanted to leave to your child. The trust can be designed so that the assets are not the property of your child, so the trust's contents do not belong to the child. Translation? The bequest is protected from future creditors or a future spouse. This trust can also distribute money to a child at designated ages so it is not inherited all at once (i.e., at 21).

There are many different kinds of trusts for lots of specific situations, but they all are variations of two larger categories: the revocable trust and the irrevocable trust.

The Revocable Trust (a.k.a., Living Trust or Grantor Trust)

The revocable trust is a bit like a will in that it is created when you are alive and it explains how the named assets are to be distributed after you die, including the precise terms for distribution (in a lump sum, as an annuity, or any other method you choose). It is *unlike* a will in that it is not a public document and it is not subject to probate and all of the administrative hassles that often accompany the probate process. The assets within the trust are simply passed to the beneficiaries upon your death. And what occurs is private; it is not a matter of public record.

One of the benefits of a living trust is that you avoid probate and all of its fees and the time delay for the distribution of your assets. However, you must re-title your assets in the name of the trust. My only caveat regarding living trusts is that because some states have a low probate cost, a trust is not always the best way to go. There are pros and cons regarding the living trust. Your CERTIFIED FINANCIAL PLANNER™ practitioner and attorney can clarify the benefits and disadvantages for you.

When you establish a revocable trust, you transfer the *title* of all of the assets you want to be included in the trust to the name you choose for the trust (e.g., The Roberta Welsh Living Trust) with your social security number, yet you (or in this case me, Roberta Welsh) maintain *ownership.* And because you are still the owner and controller of the assets, you pay tax on the income they generate. This type of trust is also referred to as a *Grantor Trust* because the person who grants the assets to the trust also retains ongoing control over it. The grantor controls the trust and is considered its trustee while he or she is living.

While you are alive, you can alter or completely revoke this type of trust (hence the name) at any time. And when you die, the revocable trust or living trust would be included in your gross estate, because you have maintained ownership of its assets.

The trustee may take over the managing of the trust if you become incapacitated, which is an important benefit. If you became incapacitated and you did *not* have a living trust or another vehicle that names a person to make decisions for you (i.e., a durable power of attorney or a living will containing a pourover provision), you would be subject to *living probate* (also known as conservatorship). In this case, someone would be appointed by the court to take control of your finances. This process can be even more expensive and more time-consuming than probate, and it can easily be avoided with the proper planning.

When you have a living trust, you provide for the management of your financial life during your lifetime as well as the management and transfer of your assets at your death. This saves the time, court fees, and attorney's fees.

The Irrevocable Trust

As the name implies, an irrevocable trust may not be altered or revoked after it is created. This is the type of vehicle that allows you to transfer *ownership* of your assets. The catch is that once you have transferred assets to an irrevocable trust, you have officially relinquished all control. The assets are no longer yours. So before you create an irrevocable trust, you want to be sure that you do not need the assets during your lifetime.

You might be thinking that you cannot imagine a reason for creating such a trust, as it is not flexible and doesn't allow for you to change your mind. However, the major advantage is that the contents of the trust will not be part of your taxable estate because they do not belong to you. This becomes a popular method for transferring funds for those who have a very large estate. This is not a good idea, however, for those whose objective is to apply for a Medicaid-eligible bed in a nursing home, because there is a 36-month up to a 60-month look back for gifted assets that would prevent Medicaid eligibility. (The laws regarding trusts for Medicaid qualification purposes are complex and have changed in recent years.)

Another rule of the irrevocable trust that you need to consider is that income taxes are paid by the trust at trust tax rates, which are more than individual rates. The decision to transfer your assets through an irrevocable trust is one with serious and permanent implications, and it should not be entered into until you have a thorough understanding of all of them.

The Irrevocable Life Insurance Trust (ILIT)

Earlier in this chapter I listed many of the assets that are included in your gross estate. One of them was "Life insurance proceeds from a policy that is owned by you or in which you have *incidents of ownership*." This means that the money you get from, say, your father's insurance company upon his death, is considered part of your estate and will be taxed if indeed you end up with a taxable estate (although you do not have to pay income taxes on the proceeds).

And the *incidents of ownership* part means that even if you are not a beneficiary, such as with your own life insurance policy, but you have *any* control over the policy (e.g., the right to cancel it, the right to change its beneficiary, the right to borrow against it), the proceeds are included in your gross estate. Essentially, if you own or have any control over *your own life insurance policy* or any other life insurance policy, the proceeds will be added in with the rest of your assets in the calculation of your gross estate.

This might sound a bit unfair to you. But it is a reality, so let's work with it. Perhaps the most important uses for your insurance proceeds are the payment of your final debts and the passing on of wealth. The money for your funeral and burial expenses, your medical expenses, your executrix and *your estate taxes need to come* from somewhere. Purchasing a life insurance policy is a way of providing liquid funds for those expenses. In a larger estate, life insurance is usually purchased for the purpose of transferring wealth. Rather than add to your estate tax burden, the policy should be owned by someone other than you. Your children could own the policy or an irrevocable life insurance trust (ILIT) could own the policy, and this would be accomplished at the time of application to the insurance company.

If on the other hand you already have a policy and now you would like to transfer ownership, if you live another three years from the date of transferring, the policy proceeds would not be included in your estate.

The transfer is technically considered a taxable gift, but its value is not equal to the death benefit. Instead, its value is tantamount to its *surrender value*. The surrender value is based on the cash value of the policy less surrender charges.

Recall that the only time a trust is not included in your estate is if it is an irrevocable trust, which is a trust that cannot be altered or "taken back" once it is established. The life insurance trust is an irrevocable trust and it should be drafted only after careful consideration of the ramifications of such an arrangement. If you choose this route you will lose ownership, hence control, of the life insurance policy you purchased. Once you transfer ownership you cannot borrow against the policy, change its beneficiary, or alter it in any other way. Any premiums for the life insurance policy are considered a gift to the owners. Be sure that your attorney counsels you on the process.

Ownership of Property

The manner in which your assets are owned will dictate what will happen to them upon your death. In some cases, this is true regardless of what you might want to state in your will, so it is important that you find out how your assets are currently owned.

Joint Tenancy

Joint tenancy is a form of ownership of property with someone else. Joint tenancy comes in two forms: *joint tenancy with right of survivorship* and *joint tenancy by the entirety*. If you and your husband own your house as joint tenants with right of survivorship, that means when the first person dies, ownership of the entire property is transferred to the survivor. This happens regardless of what is written in your will. The same is true if you and your husband own your house as joint tenants by the entirety. The only difference is that with this form of ownership, neither of you can further divide the property without the consent of the other.

Because the rules of transfer upon the death of one of the owners are built into this type of ownership, it can cause many problems. One of those problems is that you could be making unintended gifts when you die if you were planning to give the property to someone other than the person you originally held it with. In addition, if you were planning on giving your interest in the property to your husband, thereby exempting it from estate tax under the unlimited marital deduction, you cannot. *And what's more*, your estate will be taxed (if the property was transferred to a non-spouse). Essentially, this type of ownership trumps any estate planning that was to the contrary and does not give you the flexibility to choose what you want to happen with assets held this way.

Tenants in Common

This is the ownership option that gives you the most control. If you hold property as a tenant in common—even with your spouse—your estate includes your percentage of the property that you had when you were alive. You are permitted to declare to whom you would like your percentage of the property to be transferred when you pass away. This option gives you the flexibility of leaving the property to someone other than the person who owns the rest of the property. The only time it would go to your husband would be if you did not have a will or other estate planning vehicles such as a trust, and the laws of intestacy of your state say your assets would go to your husband. (There are some creditor issues to consider before changing to tenants in common, e.g., the tenants by the entirety route may offer maximum protection to the couple from creditors, which another factor to consider when deciding how to title joint assets.)

Community Property

This arrangement affects you only if you live are married and you live in one of the following nine states: Arizona, California, Idaho, Louisiana, Nevada, New Mexico, Texas, Washington, and Wisconsin. The law states that property acquired by either of you *while you are married* belongs to both of you *unless you have created a written agreement that says otherwise* (states that the property is "separate property" rather than community property).

So if you purchase some investment real estate while you are married and you are living in Texas, regardless of how you title that real estate, it belongs to your husband as much as it belongs to you. And when you die, the property will be distributed to your spouse unless you have decided otherwise and stated your intentions in your will. The property you owned prior to your marriage, that is given to you alone, or that you alone inherit, is considered separate property.

The laws of community property get complicated when you are married and you move from state to state. If, for example you move to or from Vermont, which is not a community property state (and is known as a common law state), the ownership of your property and your husband's property will change. In order to prevent any misunderstandings, review the estate planning consequences of moving *before* you move and make certain you fully comprehend them. Be sure your attorney is aware that you have lived in a community property state at some point in the past.

Gifts

If you have a sizable estate and are going to have a hefty estate tax bill, it would make sense that you should give away as much money as you can just before you die in order to avoid that bill, right?

Unfortunately, the government has already thought of that, and in an effort to prevent you from doing so, it has created a system for the taxing of individual gifts that are valued over $10,000 (as of 2001. The amount will probably increase to $11,000 by 2002).

The only time a gift valued at more than $10,000 is free from gift tax is when it is for tuition (and it is paid directly to the educational institution) or medical expenses (and they are paid directly to the institution providing the services), or when it is a spousal gift. Some states have a gift tax as well, so be sure to ask your planner if your state is one of them and how that will affect your gifting.

Although you will not annihilate your tax bill altogether
1. if you already have more than enough money to live on, and
2. you have embraced the fact that you cannot take it with you, and
3. you were planning on giving it away when you pass away, then
4. why wait until then?

Why not create a plan for gifting while you are still around to see your money being used? If you gift more than the annual exclusion of $10,000 per person, you need to file a gift tax return. There are no taxes due at this time, but the amount over $10,000 will be carried forwards until your death and then it will be subtracted from your unified credit.

The benefit of any gift, aside from enjoying the gifting, is that you will decrease your taxable estate with each gift. Ask your planner what kind of gifting plan is appropriate for you, because there are some assets that are best transferred after your death. Whether you benefit from lifetime gifting depends on your income tax bracket and whether the assets you wish to gift have appreciated in value. For instance, gifting stock that has appreciated to a church or charitable institution will allow you to reduce your estate by the current value of the stock, and also prevent you from having to pay taxes in the future if it continues to appreciate. However, gifting appreciated stock to a person means that they inherit your *cost basis*, which means that *they will have to pay capital gains taxes when they sell the stock.*

Tax-free Gifts

You can give gifts of money, jewelry, art, antiques, stocks, and all other assets that have a fair market value of up to $10,000, and not be penalized at all financially. In fact, each year you can gift money or other assets valued at up to $10,000 ($20,000 from you and your spouse), *to as many recipients as you choose.* You do not have to pay gift taxes on these gifts, they do not alter your estate tax exemption, and the recipients do not have to pay income tax on them. If that's not enough incentive, they also reduce the size of your taxable estate.

The only requirement is that each gift must be an *outright gift.* This means the person should have the right to spend the money or use the property in any way they choose, without any restrictions from you, the moment they get it. This is referred to as a "present interest" gift. The life insurance premium that is gifted to a child or an irrevocable trust can be remedied with what is known as a "Crummey Letter"; speak with your attorney about this provision.

Another transfer that is excluded from gift tax is called the *unlimited gift tax exclusion.* This states that you can pay for someone's tuition or medical expenses, including health insurance premiums, and that someone doesn't even have to be related to you. As the name implies, this gift does not have a dollar limit, although all gifts must be paid directly to the medical or educational institution providing the service to qualify.

The Unlimited Marital Deduction/Gifts to Your Spouse

The only other time a gift of over $10,000 is exempt from gift tax is when it is a transfer of an asset or assets from one spouse to the other (as long as both are U.S. citizens). This is called the *unlimited marital deduction* and it enables you, as the name says, to gift an unlimited amount of assets to your spouse during your lifetime.

The Estate Tax Marital Deduction

The estate tax marital deduction is another unlimited deduction. This one allows you to transfer as many assets as you wish, to your spouse, without either of you being required to pay gift tax. You can make the transfer while you are alive or at your death. The effect of this deduction is that you are postponing the estate tax until your spouse dies (or vice versa). Again, your spouse must be a U.S. citizen. If he isn't ask your planner for alternatives.

Technically, you could use your unified credit ($675,000) and your marital deduction if you are the first to pass away (i.e., bequeath all of your assets to your spouse), and your estate would owe nothing at your death. The problem this creates is that your spouse now has a much larger gross estate, and could have a hefty tax bill if you do not address this in your estate planning discussions as a couple.

Another benefit of the marital deduction is that the rules for how the assets are to be transferred are flexible. In other words, you can leave the assets directly to your husband in you will, which makes him the sole owner and you have no control over what happens to them next.

On the other hand, you can have them transferred to a trust that can provide for him during his lifetime, and then pass on to your designated beneficiary. This type of trust can be a QTIP Marital Trust (Qualified Terminal Interest Property Trust). All income is payable to your spouse; the principal may or may not be used by the spouse, as you wish. Alternatively, it can be structured as your Credit Shelter Trust (sometimes known as a By-Pass Trust or the Family Trust), where you have even greater flexibility as to how the income and the principal of the trust fund will be available to your spouse. In any event the key is to be sure that the trust is drafted properly so that the trust assets will count as part of your unified credit, if necessary, and any additional assets over and above the unified credit amount will be eligible for the unlimited marital deduction, discussed above.

The trust strategy is flexible in that when you create it you can do so with instructions on what should occur with your assets upon death of your spouse. In other words, this option allows you some control. So if you want to make certain that your property goes to your children when your spouse dies (and not, for example, to his next wife), you can do so with the trust.

Finalizing Your Estate Plan

Regardless of the details of your unique circumstances and the estate planning tools your planner recommends, there is one more thing that you can do after your estate plan has been created. Write a letter to be opened and read upon your death. This letter can include descriptions of all of the documents that will be needed in order to settle your estate, as well as the names, addresses, and phone numbers of all of the people who might be called upon during the process. Many financial planners offer a "document location finder" and a list of advisors with any written financial plan.

Put the letter in a safe, fireproof place in your home along with any other documents or records that will be needed in order to settle your estate in the most efficient way possible. And once all of your documents are secure, reveal their location to at least two people whom you trust.

Chapter Eight

Philanthropy

By Barbara Culver, CFP™

Karen was, by all accounts, a beautiful, successful woman. Her friends and family spoke of her in glowing terms when they recounted what she had accomplished in her career, with her family, and at home. She was thought of as well integrated, ambitious, and compassionate.

But Karen's feelings about her life—about herself—were much different. Karen felt an emptiness and a lack of fulfillment in her life, and she couldn't imagine why. After all, she had all of the visible trappings of success, and she was physically fit and beautiful. Her children were bright, sensitive, caring, individuals, and she was one of the few women she knew who was friendly with her ex-husband. Karen not only felt empty, but she also felt guilty about wanting more: wanting to fill the void. Karen was not alone.

Many women tell me that while they appear to have it all—and they are very grateful—they simply do not feel satisfied with their lives. Upon closer inspection, there are myriad reasons for this phenomenon, and most of them have one thing in common: expectations of others. Whether the expectations come from men, religion, their families, their neighbors, or the media, these women have all internalized the expectations of others. For example, advertising teaches, and society reinforces, that we will be attractive (ergo, happy) if we wear the right clothes and make-up, color our graying hair and are the proper weight for our height. Rather than following our own instincts about beauty and fulfillment, we allow outside sources to convince us that they know more about us than we do. So we internalize their advice, we follow it and we make it our own. We buy products promising we'll be beautiful, and we will never stop doing so if we think that is the answer. We find ourselves searching for the illusive feeling called happiness.

Another reason why women who appear to have it all are still not happy is because they evaluate what they have in their life (particularly the possessions) in relation to those who have more than they *have*, rather than in relation to what they *need*. In other words, though you might have everything you include in your definition of a comfortable life, you remain unhappy because so many women have so much more than you have.

The paradox here is that that which is supposed to bring happiness instead leads to suffering and even isolation. In our frenzied pursuit of things we have convinced ourselves we need, many of us have sacrificed our connection to our family and others. The result of our quest for opulence is often the most profound loneliness and emptiness.

The Solution

How then do we break out of whatever patterns we are stuck in and begin to create something new and fulfilling in our lives? There is probably a different answer for each person who asks this question. When you feel that this is something that is important for you to contemplate, here are some suggestions as to how to go about it.

1. **Focus** on yourself for a moment and ask yourself what you really want. I say focus on yourself because for many women this is not a simple task. Many women routinely put the needs of their partners, children, stepchildren, parents, parents-in-law and coworkers (especially the male ones) before their own. Too often, women have been so completely focused on others that they rarely think about what they would need to fulfill themselves. Believing that you are worthy of whatever it is that would fulfill you is of paramount importance and is primary. Once that belief is in place, you open yourself to the possibility of manifesting the very things that will fulfill you.

2. **Listen** to that little voice within you that you have ignored for so long. Realize that in order to feel fulfilled you need to respect and value that voice and follow its lead. It will help you define and refine what it is you really want. And after you have listened for awhile, make a list of the things that you now know

are necessary in order for you to truly be fulfilled.

3.   **Decide** that you have the power, abilities, and inner resources to achieve whatever is on your list. I say decide because regardless of who or what you think convinced you that you are not capable enough, good enough, or worthy enough, you chose to accept that premise and make it your own. You are not a victim forever stuck with present circumstances. Just as you have participated in the creation of your current situation, you can create a future that is very different by making different choices. Cultivating change is not easy; it requires a combination of faith, courage, and a lot of practice. But believing in yourself and knowing that you have the power to fulfill your deepest desires is essential to that work.

4.   **Seek** *new* information about whatever you believe will fulfill you. Read books, search the Internet, network, go to seminars, and join clubs. Find people who are like-minded, ask where they hang out, and go there. I stress that you seek out *new* information because much like a computer, your mind is programmable. And whether you think of it this way or not, you and your experiences have programmed your brain to handle your life in fairly predictable ways. If you are not feeling fulfilled, chances are that doing more of what you have been doing is not going to increase your sense of fulfillment. But new information and even looking at old information from a different perspective, forces you change—to do things differently. And after all, change is what you really want.

Community Capital: The Framework for Your New Self

Simply put, Community Capital is that portion of what you own and/or earn that you either choose not to keep or are not allowed to keep. For example, if you are not self-employed there is a part of every paycheck that you never receive because it belongs to the federal, state, and local governments. These taxes, as they are called, are examples of Community Capital that you are not allowed to keep.

The income tax rates are progressive, meaning the more taxable income you have, the higher the percentage you pay in taxes. But they are also cumulative, meaning that you always start at the lowest category and work your way up. For example, here are the income tax tables for a single individual for 1999.

If Taxable Income Is—

Over	but not over	the tax is		of amount over
$0	$24,000		15%	$0
24,000	58,150	$3,600.00	+28%	24,000
58,150	121,300	13,162.00	+31%	58,150
121,300	263,750	32,738.50	+36%	121,300
263,750		84,020.50	+39.6%	263,750

If you are single and you reported $60,000 of taxable income, your taxes are calculated like this:

- You owe 15% on the first $24,000 of taxable income $3,600.00
- 28% of the next $34,150 $9,562.00
- and 31% of the remaining $1,850 $573.50

So your total is $13,735.50

Here are the income tax rates for married individuals for 1999:

Married Persons Filing Jointly & Surviving Spouses
If Taxable Income Is—

Over	but not over	the tax is		of amount over
$0	$40,100		15%	$0
40,100	96,900	$6,015.00	+28%	40,100
96,900	147,700	21,919.00	+31%	96,900
147,000	263,750	37,667.00	+36%	147,700
263,750		79,445.00	+39.6%	263,750

The tax computation for a married couple filing taxable income of $105,000 works like this:

- 15% up to $40,000 $6,000
- 28% from $40,000 to $96,900   15,932
- 31% of the $8,100 balance   2,511
- Total Federal Income Taxes: 24,443

These examples represent the Community Capital part of your income that is subjected to taxation.

There is also a percentage of your estate—any amount over $675,000 if you are single and $1,350,000 if you are married—that must be shared with the government at your death before the balance of the estate can be transferred to your heirs. (That amount will gradually increase to $1 million per person by 2007.) The current Community Capital rates (tax rates) begin at 37% for your estate. This means that at least 37 cents of the first dollar of assets you own over $675,000, and every dollar thereafter, belongs to society. That leaves, at most, 63 cents of each dollar for your family. (This tax is also progressive, which means that the more you have over the $675,000 threshold, the larger the percentage society will get. At its highest level, the federal estate tax is 55% with only 45% left for your family and other heirs.)

What happens to the money from your estate that is allotted to the government? It is used to fund the federal budget as deemed appropriate by the United States Congress. This presents two problems:

1. Your estate, which took a lifetime to acquire, is quickly consumed in the federal budget.
2. Tax dollars are assigned to expenditures over which you have no control. For example, you cannot say, "Oh, by the way, please use my tax dollars to support environmental or social causes." Once the money belongs to Washington, Congress has the final say about how it will be appropriated. Therefore, a lifetime of work is transformed into dollars that not only disappear—they vanish into a budget that few people have the power to direct. In fiscal year 1999, our total federal tax dollars ($1,827 billion) were allocated in this manner:

Social Security, Medicare, and Other Retirement:	35%
National Defense, Veterans, and Foreign Affairs:	18%
Social Programs:	17%
Net Interest on the Debt:	12%
Physical, Human, and Community Development:	9%
Surplus to Pay Down the Debt:	7%
Law Enforcement and General Government:	2%

What You Can Do To Control Your Community Capital

Although you are probably aware of the workings of the federal estate tax system (described in the preceding chapter), you may not be aware that you can choose to direct your Community Capital to a recipient other than the government. While you cannot actually keep your Community Capital, you can maintain control over it rather than giving that control to the government. In fact, when thoroughly understood, the tax laws of this nation encourage us to give our taxes away!

Fulfilling Yourself by Re-directing
Your Community Capital

You can choose to spark the flame within you into a fire that represents your deepest needs and desires. And through a combination certain philanthropic and traditional estate planning tools, you can create a fire that can never be distinguished. You can leave your legacy in a way that is aligned with your life. Here are two examples of how it can be done.

The Charitable Gift Annuity

Sarah is the only child of Carol and James Smitson. James died several years ago and Carol has chosen to remain single. Unfortunately, Carol's mental acuity has been failing and she has recently been diagnosed with Alzheimer's disease. Carol, who is now seventy-five, is in excellent health and could live for decades more.

Sarah, who is fifty-five, has had an extremely successful career as a Certified Public Accountant. She never married and her life is her work. Because of the nature of her profession, Sarah has found it very easy to help her mother with all of her financial records since she was widowed. In fact, Sarah is also helping her mother make ends meet by actually paying some of her monthly expenses.

Recently, Sarah was diagnosed with a very progressive type of cancer and has been given only a few months to live. More than anything else, Sarah is worried about her mother's financial well being. It seems certain that Sarah will predecease her mother.

Sarah is aware that her estate has grown to over $2,000,000. She also knows that this means the government will receive about 50 cents of every dollar she has over $675,000 (the federal estate tax that will be due at her death). Fortunately, due to her tax training, Sarah is aware of charitable alternatives that will reduce or eliminate the enormous taxes. Sarah immediately contacts the local non-profit Alzheimer's organization and suggests a meeting with the executive director and the director of development.

At the meeting Sarah explains that her situation and that of her mother. She suggests that she take $500,000 from her estate and gift it to the Alzheimer's association in exchange for a charitable gift annuity.

A charitable gift annuity is a legally binding contract between the donor(s) and the charitable (501[c][3]) organization which creates a guaranteed income to the stated income beneficiaries for as long as either of them is alive. The charitable organization may be a university, a hospital, a medical research foundation, a family foundation, or any other qualifying charitable organization that the donor believes is worthwhile and in need. At the death of the last income beneficiary, the proceeds from the original gift belong to the charity. Here's how a charitable gift annuity works for Sarah and her mother.

> Sarah gifts $500,000 from her estate to the Alzheimer's association. This creates an income tax deduction of about $180,000 for Sarah. It also addresses her federal estate tax problem because the $500,000 is now removed from Sarah's estate. More important to Sarah, however, is that the gift annuity provides an income of $29,500 to Sarah and/or her mother for as long as either of them is alive.
>
> Sarah has given herself the gift of peace of mind to know that there is sufficient income to provide for her mother's needs, even after Sarah passes away. She also knows that, thanks to her gift, the Alzheimer's center will provide a home for her mother and will care for her.

By creatively using her Community Capital—the part of her estate that would have gone to taxes anyway—Sarah has accomplished the following:

1. She is contractually guaranteed this income will be available either to her or her mother—whomever is the survivor—for life.
2. She has saved approximately $250,000 in estate taxes.
3. She has saved approximately $55,000 in income taxes.
4. She has made a gift of the remaining annuity value to the Alzheimer's center that will help them to continue to provide care for others in perpetuity, just like they are doing for Mary.
5. By re-directing her Community Capital, she has fulfilled one her deepest desires—to provide for her mother, and then to provide for others.

The Charitable Remainder Trust

Pat and Brent Kelleher are both 67 and have been retired for several years. They are surprised to learn that in spite of their careful spending habits, they would like to have more income than their investments are currently generating.

One thing that they both want to do is travel more to see their children and grandchildren. But they feel trapped by their current investment portfolio because they will pay a huge capital gains tax if they sell the appreciated assets in the account. The account is worth $500,000 and the Kellehers' original investment was only $50,000. The significant growth in the value is due to the reinvestment of dividends and capital gains over many years.

The Kellehers' planner tells them about the most powerful and flexible estate planning tool available in the United States today, the tax-exempt Charitable Remainder Trust (CRT). This tool allows them to legally transfer the ownership of their stock from their personal account to their Charitable Trust.

The process involves making an irrevocable gift of their appreciated securities to the trust, of which they are the trustees. As the trustees, they have the power to direct the trust to sell the securities. And because the trust is tax-exempt, the stock is sold free of capital gains tax. The resulting cash can then be reinvested to generate a higher income stream for the Kellehers, which will help them meet their goals.

Moreover, the Kellehers receive a current income tax deduction of approximately $126,000, which equals about $39,000 of actual tax savings in a 31% federal tax bracket. They qualify for the income tax deduction because their money is ultimately going to a charity. So the Charitable Remainder Trust actually provides for and maintains two sets of beneficiaries: the Kellehers are the income beneficiary, and the charity of their choice is the beneficiary of the principal after the Kellehers pass away.

The income they receive will depend on the payout percentage they choose and the amount of income that their assets generate while they are inside the trust. According to the IRS, a legitimate CRT must distribute at least 5% of the value of its assets. And because the transfer of the assets is technically considered a gift, and there is no limit to the amount we can gift, there is no limit to the amount the Kellehers can transfer to their CRT.

In addition to receiving more income, avoiding paying capital gains tax, and receiving an attractive current income tax deduction, the Kellehers have also removed the $500,000 from their estate. Therefore, when their estate is assessed for possible estate taxes, the $500,000 will not be included. This could save them up to $275,000 in taxes, which they will be able to redirect to the charity(ies) of their choice.

Though there are numerous philanthropic planning tools to choose from, they all have something in common: the assets you gift to them will be used for charitable purposes, but you get to control them.

One choice you have is where to send your gifts at your death. For example, the Kellehers could choose to give the value of the assets that remain in their Charitable Remainder Trust at their deaths directly to the charity or charities of their choice. They might split the gift among *their* place of worship, the arts, and their alma maters. In this case, the money goes to these organizations where it is invested for future use.

The Charitable Lead Trust

The Charitable Lead Trust (CLT) is similar to the Charitable Remainder Trust in that it is a vehicle that benefits a charitable organization as well as the individual (or family) who establishes and funds it. It is similar also because it offers current income tax deductions and can offset capital gains taxes. The main difference is that the Charitable Lead Trust provides the charity you choose with income *while you are alive* whereas the Charitable Remainder Trust provides the charity with income *after you have died.* The charity is the income beneficiary and you, your children or grandchildren are the beneficiary(ies) of the principal.

How does the CLT work?

First, you make a donation to the trust in the form of cash, cash equivalents, or securities that typically are not highly appreciated. In return, you receive a gift or estate tax deduction, or an income tax deduction, depending on the type of trust, the ultimate beneficiary and the timeframe of the funding. The gift or estate tax deduction must be utilized in the year the trust is funded. In contrast, the income tax deduction may be used in the current year plus, if needed, five additional years.

When the trust is formed, its assets are invested in such a way that meets your individual needs as well as the distribution requirements of the trust, and includes income-producing investments such as municipal bonds. The income that must be paid out is either a percentage of the trust assets revalued annually (i.e., a Unitrust) or percentage of the trust that is fixed at the time of its funding (i.e., an Annuity Trust).

Charitable Lead Trusts typically last for a specified number of years or as long as you live. The length of time is determined by the tax benefits that you or your family will receive. When the trust ends, the remaining assets are either passed to the heirs you select or they revert back to you.

The Family Foundation

An alternative to giving money directly to charity is to choose to make a Family Foundation the ultimate recipient of the value of the charitable trust proceeds. For example, the Kellehers could establish a Family Foundation that would make annual gifts to other charities. Establishing a foundation can be as easy as filling out an application and setting some parameters for its operation, or it can be decidedly more complex. The amount of control you want over the foundation is directly related to its complexity. The beauty of the Family Foundation is that future generations of Kellehers can direct these gifts on behalf of the family. Pat and Brent's children and grandchildren can continue the legacy that began years earlier.

Let's look at what Pat and Brent can accomplish by choosing Voluntary Philanthropy (Charitable Giving) over Involuntary Philanthropy (Taxation):

1. They can avoid capital gains taxes on the sale of appreciated assets.
2. They can create the additional income they need.
3. They can remove a large asset from their estate, thereby avoiding the federal estate tax on it.
4. They can establish a family legacy that will continue into eternity.
5. They can give future generations the privilege of managing the legacy.
6. They can move from being Merely Successful to feeling Meaningfully Significant by creating this legacy.

Once thought of as a tool for only the wealthiest of the wealthy, today a Family Foundation is a technique for anyone who has either a significant estate tax problem, or simply wants to leave a legacy that their family will direct.

Today you can begin a Family Foundation with as little as $10,000. You can elect to fund the Foundation during your lifetime, at your death, or both. If funded during your lifetime, you receive a current income tax deduction for the entire $10,000 and you continue to maintain control over it, although it is no longer a part of your estate. At any time after the Foundation is funded, you may choose to give away the entire $10,000, only the interest it generates, or something in between. You can add to your Foundation at any time, and others can contribute to it as well. There is very little paperwork and even less cost to establish a public Family Foundation and it offers significant tax results. You can reduce or eliminate the Federal Estate Tax liability and also receive current income tax deductions for your gift.

Combining a Family Foundation with a Charitable Remainder Trust

Combining a Family Foundation with a CRT creates tremendous planning opportunities. While the CRT provides significant lifetime benefits, naming the Family Foundation as the charitable recipient of the proceeds of the trust adds the benefit of creating a legacy that lasts into perpetuity.

Your Journey to Leaving Your Legacy

When you begin to contemplate leaving a legacy, your first step is to ask yourself a series of simple questions about your family and your experiences with money. Some of those simple questions are listed below, excerpted from my questionnaire called *Making Peace with Money*. I promise you, however, that your responses will belie the simplicity of the questions. Without exception, my clients come away from their experience with the questionnaire with a deeper understanding of their beliefs and attitudes about wealth, family and values.

And when they have grown comfortable with their new understanding, they are ready to articulate precisely what they would like their money to do in the future, and they have a better idea of how their deepest desires can be fulfilled. The tool they use is another questionnaire I have developed, called *My Living Legacy*.

Making Peace With Money

In my experience, everyone has unique issues regarding their relationship with money. We all need to own our money mistakes as well as our triumphs. And we all need to face our money demons if we are to successfully transition from thinking about our lives to planning our legacies.

In order to begin to plan your future, you must put it into its proper context: your past and your present. Your current thoughts and feelings about wealth, family and values have their roots in your childhood. The following are some of the questions I ask my clients to contemplate before we begin our planning. If you haven't considered how influential your childhood was in the formation of your thoughts and feelings about money, take a moment to consider a sampling of the questions from *Making Peace With Money*. I'm certain they will help reveal how the environment you grew up in was filled with conversations and experiences that would inevitably contribute to your relationship with money as an adult.

1.   Where do you fit in your family's birth order?
2.   What is the best memory you have from your childhood?
3.   How do you think this memory has influenced you today?
4.   What is your most painful memory from your childhood?
5.   How do you think this memory has influenced you today?
6.   As a child, what lessons did you learn about money?
7.   From whom did you learn them?
8.   When you were growing up, who controlled the money in your household?
9.   Did you have your own money as a child?
10. If so, how did you acquire it?
     _____Worked for it
     _____Received it as gifts
     _____Got an allowance
     _____Just asked for it
11. When you remember your family, of what are you most proud?
12. When you remember your family, what are their greatest limitations?
13. Name your family's greatest priorities.
14. What do you think of those priorities today?

After you have spent some time with your memories, I suggest returning to the present and exploring your adult notions about money. Again, the following are a sampling of the questions and issues I ask my clients to reflect upon.

1. What is your unique talent or special gift?
2. Where have you put most of your time and energy so far?
3. What is the most important lesson you've learned from your life's work?
4. Which activities connected to your career have been of the greatest worth?
5. What is your most important lifetime goal?
6. How do you define success?
7. What is the most important lesson you've learned from having money?
8. What is the most important lesson you've learned from not having money?
9. What is your greatest fear in life?
10. What is missing from your life?
11. What is your greatest certainty about life?
12. From the following list of life choices, select the five that are most important to you and the five that are the least important.

Relationship with Family	Education
Relationship with Friends	Security
Relationship with God/Higher Power	Generosity
Passion	Frugality
Health	Social Status
Happiness	Loyalty
Making a Difference	Intelligence
Approval	Adventure
Acceptance	Career
Achievement	Spirituality

Next, if you have a spouse or significant other, I suggest you reflect upon that relationship. Among the issues I ask my clients to contemplate are:

1. How many times have you been married?
2. How did you meet your present spouse?
3. How are you most like your spouse?
4. In what ways are you most different?

5.   How confident are you in your spouse's ability to manage
      money after your death?
6.   How did your parents originally react to your choice for a
      spouse?

I also include a host of questions about children, grandchildren and other significant people in your life. I seek to help my clients articulate their thoughts and feelings regarding their relationships with those closest to them. For some, it is the first time they are endeavoring to do such revealing exercise. Inevitably, they reach connections between those relationships and their personal relationship with money.

Answering these questions begins to fill the emptiness many women feel because it integrates their inner self with their actions. Each of us authors our own chapter in the book of humanity. That chapter is an everlasting expression of our deepest self and it adds to the quality of the lives of others. In the moment of choice we decide between:

*   Involuntary and voluntary philanthropy
*   Taxes and gifts
*   Reactive and proactive
*   Others' way and our way
*   Getting and giving
*   Consumption and contribution
*   Success and significance

Next is a sample of questions from a questionnaire I use for legacy planning. Your answers will become a guide that reveals which people, places, causes and organizations are important to you. It will help you share your beliefs with family and explain certain provisions you would like to make for the future. It will allow you to share your hope that the people who are important to you will participate with you in life and succeed you in death in distributing your wealth in a manner that reflects your values. This legacy of living and giving philanthropically can be passed on from generation to generation as an integral part of your family tradition.

1. There are only three places your estate can go at your death. If your estate was settled today, what would be your desired percentage for each of these sections:

   IRS____% Heirs____% Charity____%
2. Would you relinquish control of assets during your lifetime if it would help accomplish your goals from the previous question?
3. Do you feel any particular responsibility or desire to conserve assets for your heirs?
4. How do you feel about gifting assets to children during your lifetime?
5. What are your beliefs about children earning their own wealth?
6. Based on your cumulative life experiences to date, what is the most important lesson you would teach your children/grandchildren?
7. Select the three areas you are most passionate about:

human rights	music	children
culture	health	environment
education	literature	athletics
business	elderly	homeless
wildlife	art	domestic
animals	religious / institutional causes	

8. If you knew someone would hang a plaque in your honor someday, where would you want it to hang, and what would you want it to say?

A professional called a Life Planner can help you interpret and integrate these two questionnaires with traditional estate planning tools to maximize the effectiveness of your estate plan. The primary goal of Life Planning is to focus on the individual's conception of her life's purpose, rather than on the accumulation of money or things. It is about shifting from an emphasis on *having* to an emphasis on *being*. Once you decide who you want to be, your Life Planner will help you create a financial plan that will turn your thoughts into realities.

When you stop giving, you begin to die.
—Eleanor Roosevelt

About the Authors

Lois Carrier, CFP™

Lois Carrier, CFP™, is a senior partner in the firm of Gilbert, Carrier, Maurice and Benzer. In addition, Lois is a registered representative offering Securities through Linsco/Private Ledger (Member NASD/SIPC). The firm is composed of a dedicated team of professionals who specialize in private asset and cash flow management. The firm's emphasis is a partnership engagement with their client in an ongoing process of education involving the protection of their wealth and cash flow preservation.

Lois' enthusiastic and motivational style of speaking is contagious and expresses her zest for life, people and her profession. She has spoken at numerous national conferences including the Institute of Certified Financial Planners, the International Association of Financial Planners and Linsco Private Ledger. She is a past member of the National Board of Directors of the Financial Planning Association.

Her unique approach to the relationship of money in each person's life makes her a popular and compelling seminar presenter. She offers advice through a weekly radio and television show and is greatly respected for her commitment to the elimination of financial illiteracy.

Lois believes that the abundant flow of prosperity from the universe is a gift to all who know how to receive it.

Lois Carrier, CFP™
Gilbert, Carrier, Maurice and Benzer, Inc.
129 W. Depot Street, Suite 10
Greeneville, TN 37743
lcarrier@gcmb.com
800-677-4445

Barbara Culver, CFP™

A principal of Resonate, Inc., Barbara Culver, CFP™ is a nationally known financial and estate planner, speaker, consultant, and author of numerous articles and the book, *Getting to the Heart of the Matter.* Unlike most professional advisors who bring a transactional approach to planning, Barb distinguishes her company with transformational planning. This process integrates all aspects of the clients' lives – financial, emotional, social and spiritual. She then aligns who people are with what they have through state-of-the-art plan design. Because Barb pioneered this "whole person" approach, she is a much sought-after industry speaker, she serves as Editor-in-Chief of the Commerce Clearing House *Journal of Practical Estate Planning*, she has appeared on CBS' "This Morning," CNBC's "Money Talk" and National Public Radio. She has also been interviewed by *Money Magazine*, the *Wall Street Journal* and *The New York Times*.

Barbara Culver, CFP™
Resonate, Inc.
4750 Ashwood Drive
Cincinnati, OH 45241
bculver@resonatecompanies.com
513-605-2500

Carter W. Leinster, CFP™

Carter W. Leinster, CFP™, ChFC, CLU, has been a financial planning consultant since 1978 and is President of Triad Financial Advisors, Inc. Carter is a member of the Financial Planning Association, an international network of financial planning firms, and a member of the Institute of Certified Financial Planners. Carter is a member of the Greensboro Estate Planning Council, the Greensboro Area Chamber of Commerce and the Professional Advisory Committee of the Community Foundation of Greater Greensboro. She has a strong interest and involvement in causes and professional organizations that involve women, two of which are the local Womens' Professional Forum, and the Girl Scouts. Carter has an MBA with a concentration in Finance from the University of North Carolina, Chapel Hill and a BA from Duke University.

Carter Leinster, CFP™
Triad Financial Advisors
333 North Greene Street, Suite 506
Greensboro, NC 27401
carter.leinster@triadfinancialadvisors.com
336-230-0071

Cicily Maton, CFP™

Cicily Maton, CFP™ is the president of Aequus Wealth Management Resources, a fee-only financial planning and asset management firm that specializes in wealth building techniques and strategies. Founded in 1987, Aequus is dedicated to helping its high net worth clients define and live more fulfilling lives. As a Registered Investment Advisor with the Securities and Exchange Commission, Ms. Maton is a proponent of behavioral finance and a recognized expert in the area of divorce planning.

Her extensive experience in money matters has made her a much sought-after writer and speaker. Ms. Maton recently wrote a book on divorce available exclusively online through CCH (Commerce Clearing House) entitled *Financial Planning Solutions.* She also has written articles for, and been quoted in, numerous magazines and media outlets including *The New York Times, Chicago Tribune, Wealth Magazine, Elle* and the *Dow Jones Investment Advisor.* Her seminars and speaking engagements for legal, business and financial organizations have taken her all across America.

Cicily Maton, CFP™
Aequus Wealth Management Resources
303 West Erie Street, Suite 311
Chicago, IL 60610
cicily@aequuswealth.com
312-664-4090

Roberta Welsh, CFP™

Roberta Welsh, CFP™ and her husband created Welsh & Welsh, located in Glen Allen, VA, in 1985. Roberta specializes in Estate Planning and Planning for Families with Special Needs. Her personal and professional dedication to helping those with special needs began when she was faced with trying to provide for the future of one her own (five) children, who was diagnosed as "mentally retarded" in 1972. Upon thoroughly researching all existing options for people with special needs, she found the system lacking and created a vehicle to provide for them, called the Commonwealth Trust in Virginia. Roberta soon became known as an advocate for those with special needs and an expert in how to plan for them. Her practice soon evolved into one concentrating on providing planning advice to families with special needs. Roberta is currently writing a book (John Wiley & Sons, Spring 2002) focusing on the many financial needs of families who have been affected by disabilities.

Roberta Welsh, CFP™
Welsh & Welsh
4551 Cox Road, Suite 110
Glen Allen, VA 23060
Rwelsh37@aol.com
804-527-7921

Index